DANDY DOGS

14 Chic Canine Crochet Projects

Kristi Simpson

LEISURE ARTS, INC. • Maumelle,Arkansas

Kristi Simpson

Inspired by her love of yarn, Kristi enjoys designing knit and crochet patterns with a fresh and modern touch. By using a mix of stitches creatively, she designs patterns that are great for beginners and beyond. She has had many books published with more in the works, featured as host in several video tutorials and been included in multiple magazines.

This book is dedicated to our sweet Claire. She was our beautiful rottweiler that kept us laughing, loving and playing tug-of-war with anything she could find. Her fun personality always lit up the room and her poots cleared the room. Her sweet snuggles, flops and grunts were the best. She was with us for almost 16 years and now rolls around on Rainbow Road. To our 'Sassy Old Lady': your stories and love will live on in our hearts forever and ever.

Look for other Leisure Arts books featuring Kristi's designs at the following address:

www.leisurearts.com/meet-thedesigners/kristi-simpson.html

Contents

PROJECTS

EASY

TANK

Up early, stretching and tying on her walking shoes, Mia is ready for her daily dog-walking job. She has a pack of 8 dogs that keeps her busy. She loves her four-legged clients and takes great care of them, even bringing them to her home for a midday break. Out the door, her daily routine begins with picking up Tank. Tank is a cheerful pup with the most adorable floppy ears. On his walk, he insists on stopping and howling at all the passing bikes and cats and dogs and...well, you get it. He likes to howl. His energy is contagious, keeping Mia on pace and the other pooches in line.

Finished Height:

Approx. 7½" (19 cm) (seated)

Yarn (Medium Weight - 4)

7 ounces, 364 yards - per skein (198 grams, 333 meters) - per skein

- ☐ Brown - 1 skein **or** 90 yards (82.5 meters)
- ☐ White - 1 skein **or** 30 yards (27.5 meters)
- ☐ Pink - 6 yards (5.5 meters)
- ☐ Dk Gray - 3 yards (2.7 meters)
- ☐ Burgundy - 2 yards (1.8 meters)

Crochet Hook

- ☐ Size G (4 mm) **or** size needed for gauge

Additional Supplies

- ☐ Polyester fiberfill
- ☐ Yarn needle

GAUGE INFORMATION

8 sc and 9 rows = 2" (5 cm)

Gauge Swatch: 2" (5 cm) square Ch 9.

Row 1: Sc in second ch from hook and in each ch across: 8 sc.

Rows 2-9: Ch 1, turn; sc in each sc across. Finish off

STITCH GUIDE

SINGLE CROCHET 2 TOGETHER ***(abbreviated sc2tog)***

Pull up a loop in each of next 2 sts, YO and draw through all 3 loops on hook ***(Fig. 8a, page 61)*****(counts as one sc).**

HALF DOUBLE CROCHET 2 TOGETHER ***(abbreviated hdc2tog)*** (uses next 2 sts)

★ YO, insert hook in **next** st, YO and pull up a loop; repeat from ★ once **more**, YO and draw through all 5 loops on hook ***(Fig. 8b, page 61)*****(counts as one hdc).**

DOUBLE CROCHET 2 TOGETHER ***(abbreviated dc2tog)*** (uses next 2 sts)

★ YO, insert hook in next st, YO and pull up a loop, YO and draw through 2 loops on hook; repeat from ★ once **more**, YO and draw through all 3 loops on hook ***(Fig. 8c, page 61)*** **(counts as one dc).**

BODY

Rnd 1 (Right side)**:** With Brown and beginning at bottom, make an adjustable loop to form a ring ***(Figs. 5a-d, page 60)***, work 6 sc in ring; do **not** join, place marker to indicate the beginning of the rnd ***(Fig. 1, page 60)***.

Note: Loop a short piece of yarn around any stitch to mark Rnd 1 as **right** side.

Rnd 2: 2 Sc in each sc around: 12 sc.

Rnd 3: (Sc in next sc, 2 sc in next sc) around: 18 sc.

Rnd 4: (Sc in next 2 sc, 2 sc in next sc) around: 24 sc.

Rnd 5: (Sc in next 3 sc, 2 sc in next sc) around: 30 sc.

Rnd 6: (Sc in next 9 sc, 2 sc in next sc) around: 33 sc.

Rnds 7-10: Sc in each sc around.

Rnd 11: (Sc in next 9 sc, sc2tog) around: 30 sc.

Rnd 12: Sc in each sc around.

Rnd 13: (Sc in next 8 sc, sc2tog) around: 27 sc.

Rnd 14: Sc in each sc around.

Rnd 15: (Sc in next 7 sc, sc2tog) around: 24 sc.

Rnd 16: Sc in each sc around.

Rnd 17: (Sc in next 6 sc, sc2tog) around: 21 sc.

Rnds 18 and 19: Sc in each sc around.

Stuff Body with polyester fiberfill.

Rnd 20: (Sc in next 5 sc, sc2tog) around: 18 sc.

Rnds 21 and 22: Sc in each sc around.

Rnd 23: (Sc in next 4 sc, sc2tog) around: 15 sc.

Rnd 24: (Sc in next 3 sc, sc2tog) around; slip st in next sc, finish off leaving an 8" (20.5 cm) length for sewing: 12 sts.

HEAD

Rnd 1 (Right side)**:** With White and beginning at nose, ch 4, sc in second ch from hook and in next ch, 3 sc in last ch; working in free loops on opposite side of ch ***(Fig. 9b, page 61)***, sc in next ch, 2 sc in next ch; join with slip st to first sc: 8 sc.

Note: Mark Rnd 1 as **right** side.

Rnd 2: Ch 1, 2 sc in same st as joining, sc in next sc, (2 sc in next sc, sc in next sc) 3 times; join with slip st to first sc: 12 sc.

Rnd 3: Ch 1, sc in same st as joining, 2 sc in next sc, (sc in next 2 sc, 2 sc in next sc) 3 times, sc in last sc; join with slip st to first sc: 16 sc.

Rnds 4 and 5: Ch 1, sc in same st as joining and in each sc around; join with slip st to first sc.

Rnd 6: Ch 1, sc in same st as joining and in next sc, 2 sc in next sc, (sc in next 3 sc, 2 sc in next sc) 3 times, sc in last sc; join with slip st to first sc: 20 sc.
Rnd 7: Ch 1, sc in same st as joining and in next 2 sc, 2 sc in next sc, (sc in next 3 sc, 2 sc in next sc) around; join with slip st to first sc, finish off: 25 sc.

Rnd 8: With **right** side facing, join Brown with slip st in same st as joining ***(Fig. 2, page 60)***; ch 1, sc in same st and in next 12 sc, (2 sc in next sc, sc in next sc) around; join with a slip st to first sc: 31 sc.

Rnd 9: Ch 1, sc in same st as joining and in each sc around; do **not** join, place marker to indicate the beginning of the rnd.

Rnds 10-13: Sc in each sc around.

Rnd 14: Sc in next 4 sc, sc2tog, (sc in next 3 sc, sc2tog) around: 25 sc.

Rnd 15: Sc in next 3 sc, sc2tog, (sc in next 2 sc, sc2tog) around: 19 sc.

Stuff Head with polyester fiberfill.

Rnd 16: Sc in next 2 sc, sc2tog, (sc in next sc, sc2tog) around: 13 sc.

Rnd 17: Sc in next 3 sc, sc2tog, (sc in next 2 sc, sc2tog) twice; finish off leaving an 8" (20.5 cm) length for sewing: 10 sc.

Thread yarn needle with long end and weave needle thru sts on Rnd 17 ***(Fig. 12, page 62)***; pull **tightly** to close hole and secure end.

Nose Stripe

Row 1 (Right side)**:** With White, ch 2, sc in second ch from hook: one sc.

Note: Mark Row 1 as **right** side.

Row 2: Ch 1, turn; 2 sc in first sc: 2 sc.

Rows 3 and 4: Ch 1, turn; sc in each sc across.

Row 5: Ch 1, turn; 2 sc in each of first 2 sc; finish off leaving an 8" (20.5 cm) length for sewing: 4 sc.

Tongue

Row 1 (Right side)**:** With Pink, ch 4, sc in second ch from hook and in next ch, 4 sc in last ch; working in free loops on opposite side of ch, sc in next 2 chs: 8 sc.

Note: Mark Row 1 as **right** side.

Row 2: Ch 1, turn; slip st in first 2 sc, 2 slip sts in each of next 4 sc, slip st in last 2 sc; finish off leaving a 6" (15 cm) length for sewing.

Lower Mouth

Row 1 (Right side)**:** With White, ch 3, sc in second ch from hook and in next ch: 2 sc.

Note: Mark Row 1 as **right** side.

Row 2: Ch 1, turn; 2 sc in first 2 sc: 4 sc.

Row 3: Ch 1, turn; 2 sc in first sc, sc in next 2 sc, 2 sc in next sc; finish off leaving an 8" (20.5 cm) length for sewing.

LEG (Make 2)

Rnd 1 (Right side)**:** With White, ch 5, sc in second ch from hook and in next 2 chs, 3 hdc in last ch; working in free loops on opposite side of ch, sc in next 2 chs, 2 sc in next ch; join with slip st to first sc: 10 sts.

Note: Mark Rnd 1 as **right** side.

Rnd 2: Ch 1, 2 sc in same st as joining, sc in next 2 sc, 2 hdc in each of next 3 hdc, sc in next 2 sc, 2 sc in each of last 2 sc; join with slip st to first sc: 16 sts.

Rnds 3 and 4: Ch 1, sc in same st as joining and in each st around; join with slip st to first sc.

Rnd 5: Ch 1, sc in same st as joining and in next 2 sc, hdc2tog, dc2tog twice, hdc2tog, sc in last 5 sc; join with slip st to first sc: 12 sts.

Rnd 6: Ch 1, sc in same st as joining and in next 2 sc, dc2tog twice, sc in last 5 sc; join with slip st to first sc, finish off: 10 sts.

Rnd 7: With **right** side facing, join Brown with slip st in same st as joining; ch 1, sc in same st and in each st around; join with slip st to first sc.

Rnd 8: Ch 1, sc in same st as joining and in each sc around; do **not** join, place marker to indicate the beginning of the rnd.

Rnds 9 and 10: Sc in each sc around.

Rnd 11: (Sc in next sc, 2 sc in next sc) around: 15 sc.

Rnd 12: Sc in each sc around.

Rnd 13: (Sc in next 2 sc, 2 sc in next sc) around; finish off leaving an 8" (20.5 cm) length for sewing: 20 sc.

Stuff foot with polyester fiberfill, leaving leg unstuffed.

ARM (Make 2)

Rnd 1 (Right side)**:** With White, make an adjustable loop, work 4 sc in ring; do **not** join, place marker to indicate the beginning of the rnd.

Note: Mark Rnd 1 as **right** side.

Rnd 2: 2 Sc in each sc around: 8 sc.

Rnd 3: (Sc in next sc, 2 sc in next sc) around: 12 sc.

Rnd 4: Sc in each sc around.

Rnd 5: (Sc in next sc, sc2tog) around; slip st in next sc, finish off: 8 sts.

Rnd 6: With **right** side facing, join Brown with slip st in same st as joining; ch 1, sc in same st and in each sc around; join with slip st to first sc.

Rnd 7: Ch 1, sc in same st as joining and in each sc around; do **not** join, place marker to indicate the beginning of the rnd.

Stuff Arms with polyester fiberfill as you work.

Rnds 8-15: Sc in each sc around; at end of Rnd 15, slip st in next sc, finish off leaving an 8" (20.5 cm) length for sewing.

EAR (Make 2)

Row 1 (Right side)**:** With Brown, ch 3, 2 sc in second ch from hook and in last ch: 4 sc.

Note: Mark Row 1 as **right** side.

Row 2: Ch 1, turn; sc in each sc across.

Row 3: Ch 1, turn; 2 sc in first sc, sc in next 2 sc, 2 sc in last sc: 6 sc.

Row 4: Ch 1, turn; sc in each sc across.

Row 5: Ch 1, turn; 2 sc in first sc, sc in next 4 sc, 2 sc in last sc: 8 sc.

Rows 6-8: Ch 1, turn; sc in each sc across.

Row 9: Ch 1, turn; beginning in first sc, sc2tog, sc in next 4 sc, sc2tog: 6 sc.

Row 10: Ch 1, turn; beginning in first sc, sc2tog, sc in next 2 sc, sc2tog: 4 sc.

Rows 11 and 12: Ch 1, turn; sc in each sc across; at end of Row 12, finish off leaving an 8" (20.5 cm) length for sewing.

TAIL

Row 1 (Right side)**:** With Brown and leaving an 8" (20.5 cm) length for sewing, ch 8, sc in second ch from hook and in each ch across: 7 sc.

Note: Mark Row 1 as **right** side.

Rows 2 and 3: Ch 1, turn; sc in each sc across; at end of Row 3, finish off leaving an 8" (20.5 cm) length for sewing.

With **wrong** side together, fold piece in half matching top of sc on Row 3 to free loops of beginning ch; sew seam, leaving remaining end for sewing; sew one end together and close **tightly**.

COLLAR

With Burgundy, ch 15, sc in second ch from hook and in each ch across; finish off leaving an 8" (20.5 cm) length for sewing.

TAG

With Dk Gray, ch 2, 4 sc in second ch from hook; join with slip st to first sc, finish off leaving a 6" (15 cm) length for sewing.

Sew Tag to center of Collar.

FINISHING

Using photo as a guide for placement, with **right** sides of all pieces facing and using long ends:

- Sew last round of Body across Rnds 10-13 of Head.
- Sew last round of Arms between Rnds 15 and 16 of Body.
- Sew last round of Legs across Rnds 6-12 of Body, having dog in a seated position.
- Sew end of rows of Tongue between Rnds 3 and 4 of Head.
- Placing center of Lower Mouth between Rnds 6 and 7 of Head and the ends of Row 3 at each side of Tongue, sew Lower Mouth in place.
- Centering last row of Nose Strip to Rnd 7 of Head and having beginning ch at Rnd 12, sew Nose Strip in place.
- Sew Ears to each side of Head across Rnds 13-16.
- Sew end of Tail between Rnds 7 and 8 on center back of Body; tack opposite end at Rnd 15.
- Place Collar around neck and sew ends together in back.
- Using satin stitch ***(Figs. 13a & b, page 62)***, add Dk Gray nose across Rnds 1-3 of Head; add Dk Gray eyes across Rnds 9 and 10.
- Using straight stitch ***(Fig. 14, page 62)***, add White 'reflection' dot to each eye.

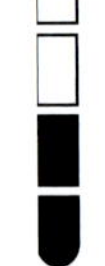

DASH

Next, Mia adds Dash to her walk. Now, Dash may have short legs, but he doesn't let that stop him from keeping up with the pack. In his mind, he's the biggest and fastest dog and she'll let him keep thinking that! Dash trots with his head and tail held high...but is ready for his water break and treats shortly after they start.

Finished Length:
Approx. 8½" (21.5 cm)

Yarn (Medium Weight - 4)
7 ounces, 364 yards - per skein (198 grams, 333 meters) - per skein
- ☐ Lt Gray - 1 skein **or** 55 yards (50.5 meters)
- ☐ Blue - 1 skein **or** 37 yards (34 meters)
- ☐ White - 22 yards (20 meters)
- ☐ Dk Gray - 22 yards (20 meters)

Crochet Hook
- ☐ Size G (4 mm) **or** size needed for gauge

Additional Supplies

- ☐ Polyester fiberfill
- ☐ Yarn needle

GAUGE INFORMATION
8 sc and 9 rows = 2" (5 cm)
Gauge Swatch: 2" (5 cm) square
Ch 9.
Row 1: Sc in second ch from hook and in each ch across: 8 sc.
Rows 2-9: Ch 1, turn; sc in each sc across.
Finish off.

STITCH GUIDE
SINGLE CROCHET 2 TOGETHER *(abbreviated sc2tog)*
Pull up a loop in each of next 2 sts, YO and draw through all 3 loops on hook *(Fig. 8a, page 61)* **(counts as one sc)**.

BODY
Rnd 1 (Right side)**:** With Lt Gray, make an adjustable loop to form a ring ***(Figs. 5a-d, page 60)***, work 6 sc in ring; do **not** join, place marker to indicate the beginning of the rnd ***(Fig. 1, page 60)***.

Note: Loop a short piece of yarn around any stitch to mark Rnd 1 as **right** side.

Rnd 2: 2 Sc in each sc around: 12 sc.

Rnd 3: (Sc in next sc, 2 sc in next sc) around: 18 sc.

Rnd 4: (Sc in next 2 sc, 2 sc in next sc) around: 24 sc.

Rnd 5: (Sc in next 3 sc, 2 sc in next sc) around: 30 sc.

Rnds 6-8: Sc in each sc around; at end of Rnd 8, slip st in next sc, finish off.

Rnd 9: With **right** side facing, join Blue with slip st in same st as slip st ***(Fig. 2, page 60)***; ch 1, sc in same st and in each sc around; join with slip st to first sc.

Rnd 10: Ch 1, sc in same st as joining and in each sc around; do **not** join, place marker to indicate the beginning of the rnd.

Rnds 11-17: Sc in each sc around.

Rnd 18: (Sc in next 13 sc, sc2tog) twice: 28 sc.

Rnd 19: (Sc in next 5 sc, sc2tog) around: 24 sc.

Rnd 20: Sc in each sc around.

Rnd 21: (Sc in next 4 sc, sc2tog) around: 20 sc.

Rnd 22: Sc in each sc around.

Rnd 23: (Sc in next 3 sc, sc2tog) around 16 sc.

Rnd 24: Sc in each sc around; slip st in next sc, do **not** finish off.

SWEATER COLLAR

Rnd 25: Ch 2 (does **not** count as a st), turn; dc in Back Loop Only of each sc around ***(Fig. 7, page 61)***; join with slip st to **both** loops of first dc.

Rnd 26: Ch 1, working in both loops, sc in same st as joining and in each dc around; join with a slip st to first sc, finish off.

Stuff Body with polyester fiberfill.

HEAD

Rnd 1 (Right side)**:** With White, make an adjustable loop to form a ring, work 6 sc in ring; do **not** join, place marker to indicate the beginning of the rnd.

Note: Mark Rnd 1 as **right** side.

Rnd 2: 2 Sc in each sc around: 12 sc.

Rnd 3: 2 Sc in each of next 6 sc, sc in next 6 sc; slip st in next sc, finish off: 18 sts.

Rnd 4: With **right** side facing, join Lt Gray with slip st in same st as slip st; ch 1, sc in same st, 2 sc in next sc, (sc in next sc, 2 sc in next sc) 5 times, sc in last 6 sc; join with slip st to first sc: 24 sc.

Rnd 5: Ch 1, sc in same st as joining and in next sc, 2 sc in next sc, (sc in next 2 sc, 2 sc in next sc) 5 times, sc in last 6 sc; do **not** join, place marker to indicate the beginning of the rnd: 30 sc.

Rnds 6-12: Sc in each sc around.

Rnd 13: (Sc in next 2 sc, sc2tog) 6 times, sc in next 6 sc: 24 sc.

Rnd 14: (Sc in next sc, sc2tog) 6 times, sc in next 6 sc: 18 sc.

Rnd 15: (Sc in next 7 sc, sc2tog) twice: 16 sc.

Rnd 16: Sc in each sc around; slip st in next sc, finish off leaving an 8" (20.5 cm) length for sewing.

Stuff Head with polyester fiberfill.

Thread yarn needle with long end and weave needle thru sts on Rnd 16 ***(Fig. 12, page 62)***; pull **tightly** to close hole and secure end.

MUZZLE

Rnd 1 (Right side)**:** With White, ch 3, 2 sc in second ch from hook, 4 sc in next ch; working in free loops on opposite side of ch ***(Fig. 9b, page 61)***, 2 sc in next ch; join with slip st to first sc: 8 sc.

Note: Mark Rnd 1 as **right** side.

Rnd 2: Ch 1, 2 sc in same st as joining, sc in next 2 sc, 2 sc in each of next 2 sc, sc in next 2 sc, 2 sc in last sc; join with slip st to first sc: 12 sc.

Rnds 3 and 4: Ch 1, sc in same st as joining and in each sc around; join with slip st to first sc.

Finish off leaving an 8" (20.5 cm) length for sewing.

LEG (Make 4)

Rnd 1 (Right side)**:** With White, make an adjustable loop to form a ring, work 4 sc in ring; do **not** join, place marker to indicate the beginning of the rnd.

Note: Mark Rnd 1 as **right** side.

Rnd 2: 2 Sc in each sc around: 8 sc.

Rnd 3: (Sc in next 3 sc, 2 sc in next sc) twice: 10 sc.

Rnd 4: (Sc in next 3 sc, sc2tog) twice; slip st in next sc, finish off: 8 sts.

Rnd 5: With **right** side facing, join Lt Gray with slip st in same st as slip st; ch 1, sc in same st and in each sc around; join with slip st to first sc.

Rnd 6: Ch 1, sc in same st as joining and in each sc around; do **not** join, place marker to indicate the beginning of the rnd.

Rnds 7-13: Sc in each sc around.

Rnd 14: Sc in each sc around; slip st in next sc, finish off leaving a 6" (15 cm) length for sewing.

Stuff end of Leg firmly with polyester fiberfill.

EAR (Make 2)

Rnd 1: With Dk Gray, make an adjustable loop to form a ring, work 4 sc in ring; do **not** join, place marker to indicate the beginning of the rnd: 4 sc.

Note: Mark Rnd 1 as **right** side.

Rnd 2: (Sc in next sc, 2 sc in next sc) twice: 6 sc.

Rnd 3: 2 Sc in each sc around: 12 sc.

Rnd 4: (Sc in next sc, 2 sc in next sc) around: 18 sc.

Rnds 5-8: Sc in each sc around.

Rnd 9: (Sc in next sc, sc2tog) around; slip st in next sc, finish off leaving an 8" (20.5 cm) length for sewing: 12 sts.

TAIL

Rnd 1 (Right side)**:** With White, make an adjustable loop to form a ring, work 4 sc in ring; do **not** join, place marker to indicate the beginning of the rnd.

Note: Mark Rnd 1 as **right** side.

Rnd 2: 2 Sc in each sc around: 8 sc.

Rnds 3-5: Sc in each sc around; at end of Rnd 5, slip st in next sc, finish off.

Rnd 6: With **right** side facing, join Lt Gray with slip st in same st as slip st; ch 1, sc in same st and in each sc around; join with slip st to first sc.

Rnd 7: Ch 1, sc in same st as joining and in each sc around; do **not** join, place marker to indicate the beginning of the rnd.

Rnds 8-11: Sc in each sc around; at end of Rnd 11, slip st in next sc, finish off leaving an 8" (20.5 cm) length for sewing.

Stuff Tail lightly with polyester fiberfill.

FINISHING

Using photo as a guide for placement, with **right** sides of all pieces facing and using long ends:

- Using free loops from Rnd 24 of Body, sew the Head to Body.
- Sew Ears to Head across Rnds 8-12.
- Sew front Legs to Body across Rnds 20 and 21; sew back Legs to Body across Rnds 8 and 9.
- Using satin stitch ***(Figs. 13a & b, page 62)***, add Dk Gray nose to Muzzle; then sew Muzzle along top of Rnd 3 of Head.
- Using satin stitch, add Dk Gray eyes across Rnds 5 and 6, leaving 5 sts between eyes.
- Using straight stitch ***(Fig. 14, page 62)***, add White 'reflection' dot to each eye.
- Sew Tail to back of Body across Rnds 2 and 3.

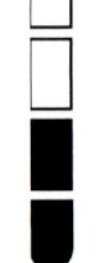

PRINCESS

Princess rules the pack and she knows it. She is always dressed in the cutest outfit…ruffled skirts, bows and even wristlets! Today, she feels even more sassy with her favorite sash wrapped around her little body. Her favorite trick is to sit…she loves her treats!

GAUGE INFORMATION

8 sc and 9 rows = 2" (5 cm)
Gauge Swatch: 2" (5 cm) square
Ch 9.
Row 1: Sc in second ch from hook and in each ch across: 8 sc.
Rows 2-9: Ch 1, turn; sc in each sc across.
Finish off.

STITCH GUIDE

SINGLE CROCHET 2 TOGETHER *(abbreviated sc2tog)*
Pull up a loop in each of next 2 sts, YO and draw through all 3 loops on hook ***(Fig. 8a, page 61)*** **(counts as one sc)**.

HALF DOUBLE CROCHET 2 TOGETHER *(abbreviated hdc2tog)* (uses next 2 sts)
★ YO, insert hook in **next** st, YO and pull up a loop; repeat from ★ once **more**, YO and draw through all 5 loops on hook ***(Fig. 8b, page 61)*** **(counts as one hdc)**.

DOUBLE CROCHET 2 TOGETHER *(abbreviated dc2tog)* (uses next 2 sts)
★ YO, insert hook in **next** st, YO and pull up a loop, YO and draw through 2 loops on hook; repeat from ★ once **more**, YO and draw through all 3 loops on hook ***(Fig. 8c, page 61)*** **(counts as one dc)**.

BODY & HEAD

Rnd 1 (Right side)**:** With Cream, make an adjustable loop to form a ring ***(Figs. 5a-d, page 60)***, work 5 sc in ring; do **not** join, place marker to indicate the beginning of the rnd ***(Fig. 1, page 60)***.

Note: Loop a short piece of yarn around any stitch to mark Rnd 1 as **right** side.

Rnd 2: 2 Sc in each sc around: 10 sc.

Rnd 3: (Sc in next sc, 2 sc in next sc) around: 15 sc.

Rnd 4: (Sc in next 2 sc, 2 sc in next sc) around: 20 sc.

Rnd 5: (Sc in next 3 sc, 2 sc in next sc) around: 25 sc.

Rnd 6: (Sc in next 4 sc, 2 sc in next sc) around: 30 sc.

Rnds 7-15: Sc in each sc around.

Rnd 16: (Sc in next 13 sc, sc2tog) twice: 28 sc.

Rnd 17: Sc in each sc around.

Rnd 18: (Sc in next 12 sc, sc2tog) twice: 26 sc.

Rnd 19: Sc in each sc around.

Rnd 20: (Sc in next 11 sc, sc2tog) twice: 24 sc.

Finished Height:

Approx. 9" (23 cm) seated

Yarn (Medium Weight - 4)

7 ounces, 364 yards - per skein
(198 grams, 333 meters) - per skein
☐ Cream - 1 skein **or** 110 yards (100.5 meters)
☐ Pink - 1 skein **or** 25 yards (23 meters)
☐ Brown - 12 yards (11 meters)
☐ Dk Gray -3 yards (2.75 meters)
☐ Lt Gray - 3 yards (2.75 meters)
☐ White - small amount

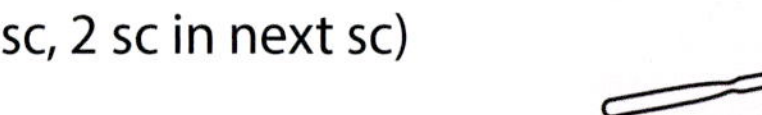

Crochet Hook

☐ Size G (4 mm) **or** size needed for gauge

Additional Supplies

☐ Polyester fiberfill
☐ Yarn needle

Rnd 21: Sc in each sc around.

Rnd 22: (Sc in next 10 sc, sc2tog) twice: 22 sc.

Rnd 23: Sc in each sc around.

Rnd 24: (Sc in next 9 sc, sc2tog) twice: 20 sc.

Rnd 25: (Sc in next 3 sc, sc2tog) around: 16 sc.

Rnd 26: (Sc in next 2 sc, sc2tog) around: 12 sc.

Rnd 27: (Sc in next 4 sc, sc2tog) twice: 10 sc.

Stuff Body with polyester fiberfill.

Rnd 28: 2 Sc in each sc around: 20 sc.

Rnd 29: (Sc in next sc, 2 sc in next sc) around: 30 sc.

Rnd 30: (Sc in next 14 sc, 2 sc in next sc) twice: 32 sc.

Rnds 31-38: Sc in each sc around.

Rnd 39: (Sc in next 2 sc, sc2tog) around: 24 sc.

Rnd 40: (Sc in next sc, sc2tog) around: 16 sc.

Stuff Head firmly with polyester fiberfill.

Rnd 41: Sc2tog around; slip st in next sc, finish off leaving an 8" (20.5 cm) length for sewing: 8 sts.

Thread yarn needle with end and weave yarn thru Front Loops Only of remaining sc *(Fig. 7, page 61)*; pull **tightly** to close hole and secure end.

ARM (Make 2)

Rnd 1 (Right side): With Cream, make an adjustable loop to form a ring, work 4 sc in ring; do **not** join, place marker to indicate the beginning of the rnd.

Note: Mark Rnd 1 as **right** side.

Rnd 2: 2 Sc in each sc around: 8 sc.

Rnds 3-9: Sc in each sc around.

Rnd 10: (Sc in next 2 sc, sc2tog) twice: 6 sc.

Rnd 11: Sc in each sc around; slip st in next sc, finish off leaving an 8" (20.5 cm) length for sewing.

Stuff Arm lightly with polyester fiberfill.

FOOT & LEG (Make 2)

Rnd 1 (Right side)**:** With Cream, ch 5, sc in second ch from hook and in next 2 chs, 3 hdc in last ch; working in free loops on opposite side of ch *(Fig. 9b, page 61)*, sc in next 2 chs, 2 sc in next ch; join with slip st to first sc: 10 sts.

Note: Mark Rnd 1 as **right** side.

Rnd 2: Ch 1, 2 sc in same st as joining, sc in next 2 sc, 2 hdc in each of next 3 hdc, sc in next 2 sc, 2 sc in each of last 2 sc; join with slip st to next sc: 16 sts.

Rnds 3 and 4: Ch 1, sc in same st as joining and in each sc around; join with slip st to first sc.

Rnd 5: Ch 1, sc in same st as joining and in next 2 sc, hdc2tog, dc2tog twice, hdc2tog, sc in last 5 sc; join with slip st to first sc: 12 sts.

Rnd 6: Ch 1, sc in same st as joining and in next 2 sc, dc2tog twice, sc in last 5 sc; do **not** join, place marker to indicate the beginning of the rnd: 10 sts.

Rnds 7-11: Sc in each st around.

Rnd 12: (Sc in next sc, 2 sc in next sc) around: 15 sc.

Rnd 13: Sc in each sc around.

Rnd 14: (Sc in next 2 sc, 2 sc in next sc) around; slip st in next sc: 20 sts.

Stuff Foot with polyester fiberfill, leaving upper part of leg unstuffed.

Joining Row: Ch 1, flatten the top of Leg with the loop on hook at the beginning and sts matching. Working through **both** loops of **both** sts, sc2tog, sc in next 6 sts, sc2tog; finish off leaving an 8" (20.5 cm) length for sewing.

MUZZLE

Row 1: With Cream, ch 4, 2 sc in second ch from hook, sc in next ch, 2 sc in next ch: 5 sc.

Row 2 (Right side)**:** Ch 1, turn; sc in each sc across.

Note: Mark Row 2 as **right** side.

Row 3: Ch 1, turn; beginning in first sc, sc2tog, sc in next sc, sc2tog: 3 sc.

Row 4: Ch 1, turn; beginning in first sc, sc2tog, using center sc again, sc2tog: 2 sc.

Trim: Ch 1, do **not** turn; sc in end of next 3 rows, sc in free loop of next 3 chs, sc in end of first 3 rows, skip last row, sc in next 2 sc on Row 4; join with slip st to first sc, finish off leaving an 8" (20.5 cm) end for sewing: 11 sc.

Stuff Muzzle with polyester fiberfill.

EAR (Make 2)

Row 1 (Right side)**:** With Brown and leaving an 8" (20.5 cm) length for sewing, ch 5, 2 sc in second ch from hook, sc in next 2 chs, 2 sc in last ch: 6 sc.

Note: Mark Row 1 as **right** side.

Rows 2 and 3: Ch 1, turn; sc in each sc across.

Row 4: Ch 1, turn; sc in first sc, 2 sc in next sc, sc in next 2 sc, 2 sc in next sc, sc in last sc: 8 sc.

Row 5: Ch 1, turn; sc in each sc across.

Row 6: Ch 1, turn; sc in first sc, 2 sc in next sc, sc in next 4 sc, 2 sc in next sc, sc in last sc: 10 sc.

Row 7: Ch 1, turn; beginning in first sc, sc2tog, sc in next 6 sc, sc2tog: 8 sc.

Row 8: Ch 1, turn; beginning in first sc, sc2tog, sc in next 4 sc, sc2tog: 6 sc.

Row 9: Ch 1, turn; beginning in first sc, sc2tog, sc in next 2 sc, sc2tog; finish off: 4 sc.

TAIL

With Brown, ch 10.

Row 1 (Right side)**:** Sc in second ch from hook and in each ch across: 9 sc.

Note: Mark Row 1 as **right** side.

Rows 2 and 3: Ch 1, turn; sc in each sc across; at end of Row 3, finish off leaving an 8" (20.5 cm) length for sewing.

With **wrong** side together, fold piece in half matching top of sc on Row 3 to free loops of beginning ch. Sew seam, leaving remaining end for sewing.

SKIRT

With Pink, ch 28.

Rnd 1 (Right side)**:** Sc in second ch from hook and in each ch across; join with slip st to first sc: 27 sc.

Note: Mark Rnd 1 as **right** side.

Rnd 2: Ch 1, sc in same st as joining and in each sc around; join with slip st to Front Loop Only of first sc ***(Fig. 7, page 61)***.

Rnd 3: Ch 5 **(counts as first dc plus ch 2, now and throughout)**, dc in same st as joining, (dc, ch 2, dc) in Front Loop Only of each sc around; join with slip st to first dc: 54 dc and 27 ch-2 sps.

Rnd 4: Ch 2 (does **not** count as a st), working in unworked loops on Rnd 2 ***(Fig. 9a, page 61)***, dc in each st around; skip beginning ch-2 and join with slip st to Front Loop Only of first dc: 27 dc.

Rnd 5: Ch 5, dc in same st as joining, (dc, ch 2, dc) in Front Loop Only of each dc around; join with slip st to **both** loops of first dc, finish off.

SASH

With Pink, ch 27.

Row 1 (Right side)**:** Working in back ridge of chs ***(Fig. 6, page 61)***, sc in second ch from hook and in next 2 chs, hdc in next ch, dc in next 18 chs, hdc in next ch, sc in last 3 chs; finish off leaving a 6" (15 cm) length for sewing.

Note: Mark Row 1 as **right** side.

WRISTLET (Make 2)

With Pink, ch 9; being careful **not** to twist ch, join with slip st to back ridge of first ch forming a ring.

Rnd 1 (Right side)**:** Ch 2, working in back ridge of chs, (slip st in next ch, ch 2) around; join with slip st to first slip st, finish off leaving a 6" (15 cm) length for sewing.

COLLAR

With Lt Gray, ch 17.

Row 1: Slip st in second ch from hook and in each ch across; finish off leaving a 6" (15 cm) length for sewing.

TAG

With Lt Grey, ch 2.

Rnd 1 (Right side)**:** 4 Sc in second ch from hook; join with slip st to first sc, finish off leaving a 6" (15 cm) length for sewing.

BOW

With Pink, ch 7.

Row 1 (Right side)**:** Working in back ridge of chs, sc in second ch from hook and in each ch across: 6 sc.

Note: Mark Row 1 as **right** side.

Rows 2 and 3: Ch 1, turn; sc in each sc across.

Finish off leaving a 6" (15 cm) length for sewing.

FINISHING

Using photo as a guide for placement, with **right** side of all pieces facing and using long ends:

- Sew Ears between Rnds 40 and 41 of Head.
- Sew Arms across Rnds 25 and 26 of Body.
- Slip Skirt onto Body, then sew Upper Leg on each side of Body across Rnds 4-11 so dog is in a seated position; tack Skirt in place.
- Sew Tail across Rnds 8-10 on lower back of Body (centered between Legs and below Skirt).
- Place center of Sash below right Arm and sew end of rows together above Left Arm; tack in place
- Wrap center of Bow with long length and then sew onto Head in front of left Ear.
- Slip Wristlet onto each Arm and tack in place on Rnd 4.
- Sew Tag to center front of Collar; then place Collar around neck and sew at back.
- Using satin stitch ***(Figs. 13a & b, page 62)***, add Dk Gray nose across center of Muzzle; using straight stitch ***(Fig. 14, page 62)***, add Gray line below center of nose.
- Sew Muzzle to center of Head, across Rnds 31-34.
- Using satin stitch, add Gray eyes across Rnds 35 and 36, having 5 sts between eyes.
- Using straight stitch, add White dot in eyes.
- Using straight stitch, add Dk Gray lashes and eyebrows.

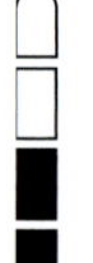

EASY

BUDDY

Buddy joins the pack and leads the way with his sniffer. Mia likes to think that Buddy would be a good police dog, but she's glad he's in her pack. She knows that his nose finds the best flowers and food trucks!

Finished Height:

Approx. 9" (23 cm) seated

Yarn (Medium Weight - 4)

3.5 ounces, 251 yards - per skein (100 grams, 230 meters) - per skein

☐ Tan - 1 skein **or** 60 yards (55 meters)
☐ White - 1 skein **or** 40 yards (36.5 meters)
☐ Black - 1 skein **or** 25 yards (23 meters)

Crochet Hook

☐ Size G (4 mm) **or** size needed for gauge

Additional Supplies

☐ Polyester fiberfill
☐ Yarn needle

GAUGE INFORMATION

8 sc and 9 rows = 2" (10 cm)
Gauge Swatch: 2" (10 cm) square
Ch 9.
Row 1: Sc in second ch from hook and in each ch across: 8 sc.
Rows 2-9: Ch 1, turn; sc in each sc across.
Finish off.

STITCH GUIDE

SINGLE CROCHET 2 TOGETHER *(abbreviated sc2tog)*

Pull up a loop in each of next 2 sts, YO and draw through all 3 loops on hook ***(Fig. 8a, page 61)*** **(counts as one sc)**.

BODY

Rnd 1 (Right side)**:** With Tan, make an adjustable loop to form a ring ***(Figs. 5a-d, page 60)***, work 6 sc in ring; do **not** join, place marker to indicate the beginning of the rnd ***(Fig. 1, page 60)***.

Note: Loop a short piece of yarn around any stitch to mark Rnd 1 as **right** side.

Rnd 2: 2 Sc in each sc around: 12 sc.

Rnd 3: (Sc in next sc, 2 sc in next sc) around: 18 sc.

Rnd 4: (Sc in next 2 sc, 2 sc in next sc) around: 24 sc.

Rnd 5: (Sc in next 3 sc, 2 sc in next sc) around: 30 sc.

Rnd 6: (Sc in next 4 sc, 2 sc in next sc) around: 36 sc.

Rnd 7: (Sc in next 5 sc, 2 sc in next sc) around: 42 sc.

Rnd 8: (Sc in next 6 sc, 2 sc in next sc) around: 48 sc.

Rnds 9-16: Sc in each sc around.

Rnd 17: (Sc in next 6 sc, sc2tog) around: 42 sc.

Rnd 18: (Sc in next 5 sc, sc2tog) around: 36 sc.

Rnd 19: (Sc in next 4 sc, sc2tog) around: 30 sc.

Rnds 20-22: Sc in each sc around.

Rnd 23: (Sc in next 3 sc, sc2tog) around: 24 sc.

Rnd 24: Sc in each sc around.

Stuff Body with polyester fiberfill.

Rnd 25: (Sc in next 2 sc, sc2tog) around: 18 sc.

Rnd 26: Sc in each sc around.

Rnd 27: (Sc in next sc, sc2tog) around: 12 sc.

Rnd 28: Sc2tog around; slip st in next sc, finish off leaving an 8" (20.5 cm) length for sewing: 6 sts.

HEAD

Muzzle

Rnd 1 (Right side)**:** With White, ch 7, 2 sc in second ch from hook, sc in next 4 chs, 4 sc in last ch; working in free loops on opposite side of ch ***(Fig. 9b, page 61)***, sc in next 4 chs, 2 sc in next ch; join with slip st to first sc: 16 sc.

Note: Mark Rnd 1 as **right** side.

Rnd 2: Ch 1, 2 sc in same st as joining, sc in next 6 sc, 2 sc in next 2 sc, sc in next 6 sc, 2 sc in last sc; join with slip st to first sc: 20 sc.

Rnd 3: Ch 1, 2 sc in same st as joining, sc in next 8 sc, 2 sc in next 2 sc, sc in next 8 sc, 2 sc in last sc; join with slip st to first sc, finish off: 24 sc.

Face

Rnd 4: With **right** side facing, join Tan with slip st in same st as joining ***(Fig. 2, page 60)***; ch 1, 2 sc in same st and in next 11 sc, sc in next 12 sc; join with slip st to first sc: 36 sc.

Rnd 5: Ch 1, sc in same st as joining, 2 sc in next sc, (sc in next sc, 2 sc in next sc) 11 times, sc in next 12 sc; join with slip st to first sc: 48 sc.

Rnd 6: Ch 1, sc in same st as joining and in each sc around; do **not** join, place marker to indicate the beginning of the rnd.

Rnds 7-11: Sc in each sc around.

Rnd 12: (Sc in next 4 sc, sc2tog) around: 40 sc.

Rnd 13: (Sc in next 3 sc, sc2tog) around: 32 sc.

Rnd 14: (Sc in next 2 sc, sc2tog) around: 24 sc.

Stuff Head with polyester fiberfill.

Rnd 15: (Sc in next sc, sc2tog) around. 16 sc.

Rnd 16: Sc2tog around; slip st in next sc, finish off leaving a 10" (25.5 cm) length for sewing: 8 sts.

Thread yarn needle with long end and weave needle thru sts on Rnd 15 ***(Fig. 12, page 62)***; pull **tightly** to close hole and secure end.

LEG (Make 2)

Rnd 1 (Right side)**:** With White, make an adjustable loop to form a ring, work 6 sc in ring; do **not** join, place marker to indicate the beginning of the rnd.

Note: Mark Rnd 1 as **right** side.

Rnd 2: 2 Sc in each sc around: 12 sc.

Rnd 3: (Sc in next sc, 2 sc in next sc) around: 18 sc.

Rnd 4: (Sc in next 2 sc, 2 sc in next sc) around: 24 sc.

Rnd 5: Sc in each sc around, changing to Tan in last sc ***(Fig. 10, page 61)***; cut White.

Rnds 6 and 7: Sc in each sc around.

Rnd 8: (Sc in next 2 sc, sc2tog) around: 18 sc.

Rnd 9: Sc in each sc around.

Rnd 10: (Sc in next sc, sc2tog) around: 12 sc.

Stuff Leg with polyester fiberfill as you work, lightly stuffing last 5 rnds.

Rnds 11-18: Sc in each sc around.

Slip st in next sc, finish off leaving an 8" (20.5 cm) length for sewing.

ARM (Make 2)

Stuffing Arm with polyester fiberfill as you work, work same as Leg leaving last 4 rnds unstuffed.

EAR (Make 2)

Rnd 1 (Right side)**:** With White, make an adjustable loop to form a ring, work 6 sc in ring; do **not** join, place marker to indicate the beginning of the rnd.

Note: Mark Rnd 1 as **right** side.

Rnd 2: 2 Sc in each sc around: 12 sc.

Rnd 3: (Sc in next sc, 2 sc in next sc) around: 18 sc.

Rnd 4: (Sc in next 2 sc, 2 sc in next sc) around: 24 sc.

Rnds 5-12: Sc in each sc around.

Rnd 13: (Sc in next 2 sc, sc2tog) around: 18 sc.

Rnd 14: (Sc in next sc, sc2tog) around: 12 sc.

Rnd 15: Sc2tog around; slip st in next sc, finish off leaving an 8" (20.5 cm) length for sewing: 6 sts.

With Tan, work second Ear.

TAIL

Row 1: With Tan, ch 10; sc in second ch from hook and in each ch across: 9 sc.

Rows 2 and 3: Ch 1, turn; sc in each sc across.

Finish off leaving a 10" (25.5 cm) length for sewing.

Fold piece in half having **wrong** side of Row 3 and free loops of beginning ch together; sew seam, leaving remaining end for sewing; sew one end together and close **tightly**.

COLLAR

With Black, ch 16, hdc in second ch from hook and in each ch across; finish off leaving a 6" (15 cm) length for sewing.

TAG

With Black, ch 2, 5 hdc in second ch from hook; join with slip st to first hdc, finish off leaving a 6" (15 cm) length for sewing.

FINISHING

Using photo as a guide for placement, with **right** sides of all pieces facing and using long ends:

- Sew Ears to Head, across Rnds 11 and 12, having 7 sts between Ears.
- On opposite side of Ears, sew Head to Body across Rnds 9-12.
- Sew Legs to Body across Rnds 11-15, so that dog is in a seated position.
- Sew top of Arms to Rnd 25 of Body; tack Arms to side at Rnd 18 if desired.
- Sew Tail to Body across Rnds 8 and 9.
- Sew Collar around Neck.
- Sew Tag to Collar.
- Using satin stitch ***(Figs. 13a & b, page 62)***, add Black nose to Muzzle.
- Using satin stitch, add Black eyes across Rnds 5 and 6, leaving 4 to 5 sts between eyes.
- Using straight stitch ***(Fig. 14, page 62)***, add White 'reflection' dot to each eye.
- Using straight stitch, add Black eyebrow over each eye.

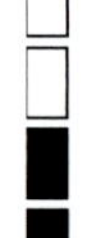

JUNIOR PUP

Junior has the softest fur and floppiest ears. He has such a relaxed personality and fits right into the pack. He loves belly rubs and sleeping after a long walk. His favorite treat is barbeque chips...but shhhh, don't tell the others he gets this secret snack!

GAUGE INFORMATION

6 sc and 5 rows = 2" (5 cm)
Gauge Swatch: 2" (5 cm) square
Ch 7.
Row 1: Sc in second ch from hook and in each ch across: 12 sc.
Rows 2-5: Ch 1, turn; sc in each sc across.
Finish off.

STITCH GUIDE

SINGLE CROCHET 2 TOGETHER ***(abbreviated sc2tog)***
Pull up a loop in each of next 2 sts, YO and draw through all 3 loops on hook *(Fig. 8a, page 61)* **(counts as one sc)**.

DOUBLE CROCHET 3 TOGETHER ***(abbreviated dc3tog)***
(uses next 3 sts)
★ YO, insert hook in **next** st, YO and pull up a loop, YO and draw through 2 loops on hook; repeat from ★ 2 times **more**, YO and draw through all 4 loops on hook **(counts as one dc)**.

BODY & HEAD

Rnd 1 (Right side)**:** With Tan, make an adjustable loop to form a ring ***(Figs. 5a-d, page 60)***, work 6 sc in ring; do **not** join, place marker to indicate the beginning of the rnd ***(Fig. 1, page 60)***.

Note: Loop a short piece of yarn around any stitch to mark Rnd 1 as **right** side.

Rnd 2: 2 Sc in each sc around: 12 sc.

Rnd 3: (Sc in next sc, 2 sc in next sc) around: 18 sc.

Rnd 4: (Sc in next 2 sc, 2 sc in next sc) around: 24 sc.

Rnd 5: (Sc in next 3 sc, 2 sc in next sc) around: 30 sc.

Rnd 6: (Sc in next 4 sc, 2 sc in next sc) around: 36 sc.

Rnds 7-12: Sc in each sc around.

Rnd 13: (Sc in next 4 sc, sc2tog) around: 30 sc.

Rnd 14: (Sc in next 3 sc, sc2tog) around: 24 sc.

Rnd 15: Sc in each sc around.

Stuff Body with polyester fiberfill.

Rnd 16: (Sc in next 2 sc, sc2tog) around: 18 sc.

Finished Height:

Approx. 9" (23 cm) seated

Yarn

(Super Bulky Weight - 6)

3.5 ounces, 131 yards - per skein (100 grams, 120 meters) - per skein
☐ Tan - 1 skein
☐ Black - 1 skein
☐ Cream - 1 skein

Crochet Hook

☐ Size H (5 mm) **or** size needed for gauge

Additional Supplies

☐ Polyester fiberfill
☐ Yarn needle

Rnds 17 and 18: Sc in each sc around.

Rnd 19: (Sc in next sc, sc2tog) around: 12 sc.

Rnd 20: 2 Sc in each sc around: 24 sc.

Rnd 21: (Sc in next 2 sc, 2 sc in next sc): 32 sc.

Rnds 22-24: Sc in each sc around.

Rnd 25: (Sc in next 6 sc, sc2tog) around: 28 sc.

Rnd 26: (Sc in next 5 sc, sc2tog) around: 24 sc.

Rnds 27 and 28: Sc in each sc around.

Rnd 29: (Sc in next 2 sc, sc2tog) around: 18 sc.

Stuff Head firmly with polyester fiberfill.

Rnd 30: (Sc in next sc, sc2tog) around; slip st in next sc, finish off leaving a 10" (25.5 cm) length for sewing: 12 sc.

MUZZLE

Rnd 1 (Right side)**:** With Black, ch 4, 2 sc in second ch from hook, sc in next ch, 4 sc in last ch; working in free loops on opposite side of ch ***(Fig. 9b, page 61)***, sc in next ch, 2 sc in next ch; join with slip st to first sc: 10 sc.

Note: Mark Rnd 1 as **right** side.

Rnd 2: Ch 1, 2 sc in same st as joining, sc in next 3 sc, 2 sc in each of next 2 sc, sc in next 3 sc, 2 sc in last sc; join with slip st to first sc: 14 sc.

Rnd 3: Ch 1, 2 sc in same st as joining, sc in next 5 sc, 2 sc in each of next 2 sc, sc in next 5 sc, 2 sc in last sc; join with slip st to first sc: 18 sc.

Rnd 4: Ch 1, sc in same st as joining and in each sc around; join with slip st to first sc, finish off leaving a 12" (30.5 cm) length for sewing.

BACK LEG (Make 2)

Rnd 1 (Right side)**:** With Black, make an adjustable loop to form a ring, work 6 sc in ring; do **not** join, place marker to indicate the beginning of the rnd.

Note: Mark Rnd 1 as **right** side.

Rnd 2: 2 Sc in each sc around: 12 sc.

Rnd 3: Sc in each sc around.

Rnd 4: Sc in next 3 sts, dc3tog twice, sc in next 3 sts: 8 sts.

Rnds 5-7: Sc in each st around.

Rnd 8: Sc in each sc around, changing to Tan in last sc ***(Fig. 10, page 61)***; cut Black.

Stuff Leg with polyester fiberfill as you work, lightly stuffing last 5 rnds.

Rnds 9-13: Sc in each sc around; at end of Rnd 13, slip st in next sc, finish off leaving an 8" (20.5 cm) length for sewing.

FRONT LEG (Make 2)

Stuffing Front Leg with polyester fiberfill as you work, work same as Back Leg leaving last 5 rnds unstuffed.

EAR (Make 2)

Row 1: With Tan, ch 2, 2 sc in second ch from hook.

Row 2 (Right side)**:** Ch 1, turn; sc in each sc across.

Note: Mark Row 2 as **right** side.

Row 3: Ch 1, turn; 2 sc in each sc across: 4 sc.

Row 4: Ch 1, turn; 2 sc in first sc, sc in next 2 sc, 2 sc in last sc: 6 sc.

Rows 5 and 6: Ch 1, turn; sc in each sc across.

Finish off leaving a 10" (25.5 cm) length for sewing.

Edging: With **right** side facing and working in end of rows, join Black with sc in end of Row 6 ***(Fig. 3, page 60)***; sc in next 4 rows, skip next row; (sc, ch 1, sc) in free loop of beginning ch; working in end of rows, skip first row, sc in last 5 rows; finish off.

EYE (Make 2)

Rnd 1 (Right side)**:** With Black, make an adjustable loop to form a ring, work 4 sc in ring; join with slip st to first sc, finish off leaving an 8" (20.5 cm) length for sewing.

TAIL

Rnd 1 (Right side)**:** With Black, make an adjustable loop to form a ring, work 4 sc in ring; join with slip st to first sc.

Note: Mark Rnd 1 as **right** side.

Rnd 2: Ch 1, sc in same st as joining and in last 3 sc; do **not** join, place marker to indicate the beginning of the rnd.

Rnd 3: Sc in each sc around, changing to Tan in last sc, cut Black.

Rnds 4-9: Sc in each sc around; at end of Rnd 9, slip st in next sc, finish off leaving an 8" (20.5 cm) length for sewing.

COLLAR

With Cream, ch 16, hdc in second ch from hook and in each ch across; finish off leaving a 6" (15 cm) length for sewing.

TAG

With Cream, ch 2, 5 hdc in second ch from hook; join with slip st to first hdc, finish off leaving a 6" (15 cm) length for sewing.

Thread needle with long end on Tag and sew to center of Collar.

FINISHING

Using photos as a guide for placement, with **right** sides of all pieces facing and using long ends:

- Sew Ears to Head, across Rnds 26-30.
- Sew Back Legs across Rnds 5-7 of Body so dog is in a seated position.
- Centering Front Legs, sew to Body between Rnds 18 and 19.
- Sew Tail to Body, across Rnds 7 and 8.
- Sew Muzzle across Rnds 22-25.
- Using satin stitch ***(Figs. 13a & b, page 62)***, add Tan nose to Muzzle.
- Sew Collar around Neck.
- Using straight stitch ***(Fig. 14, page 62)***, add Tan 'reflection' dot to each eye.

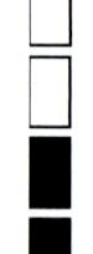

DEXTER

Dexter is an active dog. He loves to play fetch and if you're not careful…he'll steal any ball he finds! This makes for an interesting walk through the park. Dexter is a good boy that stays in line and never causes any trouble (except stealing balls!).

Finished Height:
Approx. 7" (18 cm) seated

Yarn (Medium Weight - 4)
7 ounces, 364 yards - per skein
(198 grams, 333 meters) - per skein
- ☐ Brown - 1 skein
- ☐ Blue - 1 skein
- ☐ Dk Gray - 1 skein
- ☐ Burgundy - small amount
- ☐ Pink - small amount
- ☐ White - small amount

Crochet Hook
☐ Size G (4 mm) **or** size needed for gauge

Additional Supplies

- ☐ Polyester fiberfill
- ☐ Yarn needle

GAUGE INFORMATION
8 sc and 9 rows = 2" (5 cm)
Gauge Swatch: 2" (5 cm) square
Ch 9.
Row 1: Sc in second ch from hook and in each ch across: 8 sc.
Rows 2-9: Ch 1, turn; sc in each sc across.
Finish off.

STITCH GUIDE
SINGLE CROCHET 2 TOGETHER ***(abbreviated sc2tog)***
Pull up a loop in each of next 2 sts, YO and draw through all 3 loops on hook ***(Fig. 8a, page 61)*** **(counts as one sc)**.

LEGS
First Leg
Rnd 1 (Right side)**:** With Brown, make an adjustable loop to form a ring ***(Figs. 5a-d, page 60)***, work 5 sc in ring; do **not** join, place marker to indicate the beginning of the rnd ***(Fig. 1, page 60)***.

Note: Loop a short piece of yarn around any stitch to mark Rnd 1 as **right** side.

Rnd 2: 2 Sc in each sc around: 10 sc.

Rnds 3-6: Sc in each sc around; at end of Rnd 6, slip st in next sc, finish off.

Rnd 7: With **right** side facing, join Blue with slip st in same st as joining ***(Fig. 2, page 60)***; ch 1, working in Front Loops Only ***(Fig. 7, page 61)***, slip st in each sc around; join with slip st to first slip st: 10 slip sts.

Rnd 8: Ch 1, working in Back Loops Only ***(Fig. 7, page 61)***, sc in each slip st around; join with slip st to **both** loops of first sc.

Rnd 9: Ch 1, sc in same st as joining and in next 3 sc, 2 sc in next sc, sc in next 4 sc, 2 sc in next sc; join with slip st to first sc: 12 sc.

Rnd 10: Ch 1, sc in same st as joining and in next 2 sc, 2 sc in next sc, (sc in next 3 sc, 2 sc in next sc) twice; join with slip st to first sc, finish off: 15 sc.

Second Leg

Work same as First Leg; do **not** finish off.

Stuff Legs with polyester fiberfill.

BODY

Rnd 1 (Right side)**:** Working on same Leg, ch 1, sc in same st as joining and in each sc around; working in sts on First Leg, sc in each st around; do **not** join, place marker to indicate the beginning of the rnd: 30 sc.

Note: Mark Rnd 1 as **right** side.

Rnds 2-8: Sc in each sc around; at end of Rnd 8, slip st in next sc, finish off.

Rnd 9: With **right** side facing, join Brown with slip st in same st as joining; ch 1, working in Back Loops Only, sc in same st and in each sc around; join with slip st to **both** loops of first sc.

Rnd 10: Ch 1, working in both loops, sc in same st as joining and in each sc around; do **not** join, place marker to indicate the beginning of the rnd.

Rnds 11 and 12: Sc in each sc around.

Rnd 13: (Sc in next 3 sc, sc2tog) around: 24 sc.

Rnd 14: Sc in each sc around.

Rnd 15: (Sc in next 2 sc, sc2tog) around: 18 sc.

Rnd 16: Sc in each sc around.

Rnd 17: (Sc in next sc, sc2tog) around: 12 sc.

Rnd 18: (Sc in next 4 sc, sc2tog) twice; do **not** finish off: 10 sc.

Stuff Body firmly with polyester fiberfill.

HEAD

Rnd 1: 2 Sc in each sc around: 20 sc.

Rnd 2: (Sc in next sc, 2 sc in next sc) around: 30 sc.

Rnd 3: (Sc in next 14 sc, 2 sc in next sc) twice: 32 sc.

Rnds 4-10: Sc in each sc around.

Rnd 11: (Sc in next 2 sc, sc2tog) around: 24 sc.

Rnd 12: (Sc in next sc, sc2tog) around: 16 sc.

Stuff Head firmly with polyester fiberfill.

Rnd 13: Sc2tog around; slip st in next sc, finish off leaving an 8" (20.5 cm) length for sewing: 8 sts.

Thread yarn with long end and weave needle thru sts on Rnd 13 ***(Fig. 12, page 62)***; pull **tightly** to close hole and secure end.

ARM (Make 2)

Rnd 1 (Right side)**:** With Brown, make an adjustable loop to form a ring, work 4 sc in ring; do **not** join, place marker to indicate the beginning of the rnd.

Note: Mark Rnd 1 as **right** side.

Rnd 2: 2 Sc in each sc around: 8 sc.

Rnds 3-9: Sc in each sc around.

Rnd 10: (Sc in next 2 sc, sc2tog) twice: 6 sc.

Rnd 11: Sc in each sc around; slip st in next sc, finish off leaving an 8" (20.5 cm) length for sewing.

Stuff Arm lightly with polyester fiberfill.

MUZZLE

Row 1 (Right side)**:** With Brown, ch 2, 5 sc in second ch from hook: 5 sc.

Note: Mark Row 1 as **right** side.

Row 2: Ch 1, turn; 2 sc in each sc across: 10 sc.

Row 3: Ch 1, turn; sc in first sc, 2 sc in next sc, sc in next sc, 2 sc in next sc, sc in next 2 sc, (2 sc in next sc, sc in next sc) twice: 14 sc.

Rows 4 and 5: Ch 1, turn; sc in each sc across.

Finish off leaving an 8" (20.5 cm) length for sewing.

Lower Mouth

Rnd 1 (Right side)**:** With Brown, ch 2, 4 sc in second ch from hook; join with slip st to first sc: 4 sc.

Note: Mark Rnd 1 as **right** side.

Rnd 2: Ch 1, 2 sc in same st as joining and in each sc around; join with slip st to first sc: 8 sc.

Rnd 3: Ch 1, sc in same st as joining, 2 sc in next sc, (sc in next sc, 2 sc in next sc) around; join with slip st to first sc: 12 sc.

Rnd 4: Ch 1, sc in same st as joining and in next sc, 2 sc in next sc, (sc in next 2 sc, 2 sc in next sc) around; join with slip st to first sc, finish off leaving an 8" (20.5 cm) length for sewing: 16 sc.

Tongue

Row 1: With Pink, ch 2, 4 sc in second ch from hook: 4 sc.

Row 2 (Right side)**:** Ch 1, turn; sc in first sc, 2 sc in each of next 2 sc, sc in last sc; finish off leaving an 8" (20.5 cm) length for sewing: 6 sc.

Note: Mark Row 2 as **right** side.

EAR (Make 2)

Row 1 (Right side)**:** With Dark Gray, ch 3, 2 sc in second ch from hook and in last ch: 4 sc.

Note: Mark Row 1 as **right** side.

Row 2: Ch 1, turn; 2 sc in first sc, sc in next 2 sc, 2 sc in last sc: 6 sc.

Row 3: Ch 1, turn; 2 sc in first sc, sc in next 4 sc, 2 sc in last sc: 8 sc.

Rows 4 and 5: Ch 1, turn; sc in each sc across.

Trim: Ch 1, do **not** turn; working in end of rows, sc evenly across to Row 1; working in free loops of beginning ch ***(Fig. 9b, page 61)***, 2 sc in first ch, ch 1, 2 sc in next ch; working in ends of rows, sc evenly across to Row 5; join with slip st to first sc, finish off leaving an 8" (20.5 cm) length for sewing.

Fold each end of Row 5 to center and sew in place.

TAIL

Rnd 1 (Right side)**:** With Brown, make an adjustable loop to form a ring, work 4 sc in ring; do **not** join, place marker to indicate the beginning of the rnd.

Note: Mark Rnd 1 as **right** side.

Rnd 2: (2 Sc in next sc, sc in next sc) twice; slip st in next sc, finish off leaving an 8" (20.5 cm) length for sewing: 6 sts.

BOW TIE

Row 1 (Right side)**:** With Burgundy, ch 6, sc in back ridge of second ch from hook and each ch across ***(Fig. 6, page 61)***: 5 sc.

Note: Mark Row 1 as **right** side.

Rows 2 and 3: Ch 1, turn; sc in each sc across; at end of Row 3, finish off.

Cut an 8" (20.5 cm) length of Burgundy and wrap several times **tightly** around center of piece; knot ends at back of Bow Tie, leaving ends long for sewing.

SUSPENDER (Make 2)

With Blue, ch 18; finish off leaving a 6" (15 cm) length for sewing.

FINISHING

Using photo as a guide for placement, with **right** sides of all pieces facing and using long ends:

- Sew Arms to each side between Rnds 15 and 16 of Body.
- Sew Ears to each side of Head across Rnds 28-31.
- Sew beginning end of each Suspender to free loop on Rnd 8 on front of Body, leaving 4 loops between each. Crossing Suspenders at back, sew other end of each suspender to free loop on back of Body, leaving 6 loops between each.
- Flatten Lower Mouth, having sts on last rnd matching; sew to Rnd 21 of Head.
- Placing center of Rnd 5 of Muzzle at Rnd 26 of Head (centered above Lower Mouth), sew Muzzle to Head having end of rows meeting the fold on each side of Lower Mouth.
- Sew Tongue to center of Lower Mouth; stuff Muzzle then sew end of rows to each side of Lower Mouth.
- Sew Tail across Rnds 4 and 5 of center back of Body.
- Sew Bow Tie to neck.
- Using satin stitch ***(Figs. 13a & b, page 62)***, add Dark Gray nose to Muzzle.
- Using satin stitch, add Dark Gray eyes across Rnds 27 and 28.
- Using straight stitch ***(Fig. 14, page 62)***, add White 'reflection' dot to each eye.

EASY

MAX

If you get distracted, you'll lose Max. He is mischievous and will sneak away to find treats. His owners put a colorful sweater on him so he's easy to spot.... Mia stays on guard to keep up with all 8 dogs, but especially Max!

Finished Height:

Approx. 8¼" (21 cm) (seated)

Yarn (Medium Weight - 4)

7 ounces, 364 yards - per skein
(198 grams, 333 meters) - per skein

- ☐ White - 1 skein
- ☐ Green - 1 skein
- ☐ Black - 1 skein
- ☐ Lt Gray - small amount

Crochet Hook

☐ Size G (4 mm) **or** size needed for gauge

Additional Supplies

- ☐ Polyester fiberfill
- ☐ Yarn needle

GAUGE INFORMATION

8 sc and 9 rows = 2" (5 cm)
Gauge Swatch: 2" (5 cm) square
Ch 9.
Row 1: Sc in second ch from hook and in each ch across: 8 sc.
Rows 2-9: Ch 1, turn; sc in each sc across.
Finish off.

STITCH GUIDE

SINGLE CROCHET 2 TOGETHER ***(abbreviated sc2tog)***
Pull up a loop in each of next 2 sts, YO and draw through all 3 loops on hook ***(Fig. 8a, page 61)*** **(counts as one sc)**.

BODY

Rnd 1 (Right side)**:** With White, make an adjustable loop to form a ring ***(Figs. 5a-d, page 60)***, work 6 sc in ring; do **not** join, place marker to indicate the beginning of the rnd ***(Fig. 1, page 60)***.

Note: Loop a short piece of yarn around any stitch to mark Rnd 1 as **right** side.

Rnd 2: 2 Sc in each sc around: 12 sc.

Rnd 3: (Sc in next sc, 2 sc in next sc) around: 18 sc.

Rnd 4: (Sc in next 2 sc, 2 sc in next sc) around: 24 sc.

Rnd 5: (Sc in next 3 sc, 2 sc in next sc) around: 30 sc.

Rnd 6: (Sc in next 4 sc, 2 sc in next sc) around: 36 sc.

Rnds 7-10: Sc in each sc around; at end of Rnd 10, slip st in next sc, finish off.

Rnd 11: With **right** side facing, join Green with slip st in same st as slip st ***(Fig. 2, page 60)***; ch 1, sc in same st and in each sc around; do **not** join, place marker to indicate the beginning of the rnd.

Rnds 12-14: Sc in each sc around.

Rnd 15: (Sc in next 10 sc, sc2tog) around: 33 sc.

Rnd 16: Sc in each sc around.

Stuff Body with polyester fiberfill.

Rnd 17: (Sc in next 9 sc, sc2tog) around: 30 sc.

Rnd 18: Sc in each sc around.

Rnd 19: (Sc in next 8 sc, sc2tog) around: 27 sc.

Rnd 20: Sc in each sc around.

Rnd 21: (Sc in next 7 sc, sc2tog) around: 24 sc.

Rnd 22: Sc in each sc around.

Rnd 23: (Sc in next 6 sc, sc2tog) around: 21 sts.

Rnd 24: Sc in each sc around.

Rnd 25: (Sc in next 5 sc, sc2tog) around: 18 sc.

Stuff Body with polyester fiberfill.

Rnd 26: Sc in each sc around; slip st in next sc, finish off.

Rnd 27: With **right** side facing, join White with slip st in same st as slip st; ch 1, sc in same st and in next 6 sc, sc2tog, sc in next 7 sc, sc2tog; join with slip st to next sc: 16 sc.

Rnd 28: Ch 1, sc in same st as joining and in next sc, sc2tog, (sc in next 2 sc, sc2tog) around; join with slip st to first sc, finish off leaving an 8" (20.5 cm) length for sewing: 12 sts.

HEAD

Rnd 1 (Right side)**:** With White and beginning at base of Head, make an adjustable loop to form a ring, work 6 sc in ring; do **not** join, place marker to indicate the beginning of the rnd.

Note: Mark Rnd 1 as **right** side.

Rnd 2: 2 Sc in each sc around: 12 sc.

Rnd 3: (Sc in next sc, 2 sc in next sc) around: 18 sc.

Rnd 4: (Sc in next 2 sc, 2 sc in next sc) around: 24 sc.

Rnd 5: (Sc in next 3 sc, 2 sc in next sc) around: 30 sc.

Rnd 6: (Sc in next 4 sc, 2 sc in next sc) around: 36 sc.

Rnds 7-12: Sc in each sc around.

Rnd 13: (Sc in next 4 sc, sc2tog) around: 30 sc.

Rnd 14: (Sc in next 3 sc, sc2tog) around: 24 sc.

Rnd 15: (Sc in next 2 sc, sc2tog) around: 18 sc.

Rnd 16: (Sc in next sc, sc2tog) around: 12 sc.

Rnd 17: (Sc in next sc, sc2tog) around; slip st in next sc, finish off leaving an 8" (20.5 cm) length for sewing: 8 sts.

Stuff Head with polyester fiberfill.

Thread yarn needle with long end and weave needle thru sts on Rnd 15 ***(Fig. 12, page 62)***; pull **tightly** to close hole and secure end.

ARM (Make 2)

Rnd 1 (Right side)**:** With Black, make an adjustable loop to form a ring, work 4 sc in ring; do **not** join, place marker to indicate the beginning of the rnd.

Note: Mark Rnd 1 as **right** side.

Rnd 2: 2 Sc in each sc around: 8 sc.

Rnd 3: (Sc in next sc, 2 sc in next sc) around: 12 sc.

Rnd 4: Sc in each sc around.

Rnd 5: (Sc in next sc, sc2tog) around; slip st in next sc, finish off: 8 sts.

Rnd 6: With **right** side facing, join Green with slip st in same st as slip st; ch 1, sc in same st and in each sc around; join with slip st to first sc.

Rnd 7: Ch 1, sc in same st as joining and in each sc around; do **not** join, place marker to indicate the beginning of the rnd.

Stuff Arm with polyester fiberfill.

Rnds 8-14: Sc in each sc around.

Rnd 15: (Sc in next 2 sc, sc2tog) twice; slip st in next sc, finish off leaving an 8" (20.5 cm) length for sewing: 6 sts.

LEG (Make 2)

Rnd 1 (Right side)**:** With Black, make an adjustable loop to form a ring, work 4 sc in ring; do **not** join, place marker to indicate the beginning of the rnd.

Note: Mark Rnd 1 as **right** side.

Rnd 2: 2 Sc in each sc around: 8 sc.

Rnd 3: (Sc in next sc, 2 sc in next sc) around: 12 sc.

Rnd 4: (Sc in next 2 sc, 2 sc in next sc) around: 16 sc.

Rnd 5: (Sc in next 2 sc, sc2tog) around: 12 sc.

Rnd 6: (Sc in next 4 sc, sc2tog) twice; slip st in next sc, finish off: 10 sts.

Rnd 7: With **right** side facing, join White with slip st in same st as slip st; ch 1, sc in same st and in each sc around; join with slip st to first sc.

Rnd 8: Ch 1, sc in same st as joining and in each sc around; do **not** join, place marker to indicate the beginning of the rnd.

Rnds 9-14: Sc in each sc around.

Stuff Leg with polyester fiberfill.

Rnd 15: (Sc in next 3 sc, sc2tog) twice; slip st in next sc, finish off leaving an 8" (20.5 cm) length for sewing: 8 sts.

MUZZLE

Rnd 1 (Right side)**:** With White, make an adjustable loop to form a ring, work 4 sc in ring; do **not** join, place marker to indicate the beginning of the rnd.

Note: Mark Rnd 1 as **right** side.

Rnd 2: 2 Sc in each sc around: 8 sc.

Rnd 3: (Sc in next sc, 2 sc in next sc) around: 12 sc.

Rnd 4: (Sc in next 2 sc, 2 sc in next sc) around: 16 sc.

Rnd 5: (Sc in next 2 sc, sc2tog) around; slip st in next sc, finish off leaving an 8" (20.5 cm) length for sewing: 12 sts.

Stuff Muzzle with polyester fiberfill.

NOSE

Rnd 1 (Right side)**:** With Black, make an adjustable loop to form a ring, work 4 sc in ring; join with slip st to first sc: 4 sc.

Note: Mark Rnd 1 as **right** side.

Rnd 2: Ch 1, 2 sc in same st as joining, sc in next sc, 2 sc in next sc, sc in next sc; join with slip st to first sc, finish off leaving a 6" (15 cm) length for sewing: 6 sc.

Stuff Nose with polyester fiberfill.

EAR (Make 2)

Rnd 1: With Black, make an adjustable loop to form a ring, work 6 sc in ring; do **not** join, place marker to indicate the beginning of the rnd.

Note: Mark Rnd 1 as **right** side.

Rnd 2: 2 Sc in each sc around: 12 sc.

Rnd 3: (Sc in next sc, 2 sc in next sc) around: 18 sc.

Rnds 4 and 5: Sc in each sc around.

Rnd 6: (Sc2tog, sc in next sc) around: 12 sc.

Rnds 7 and 8: Sc in each sc around.

Rnd 9: Sc2tog around: 6 sc.

Rnd 10: Sc in each sc around; slip st in next sc, finish off leaving a 8" (20.5 cm) length for sewing.

FINISHING

Using photo as a guide for placement, with **right** sides of all pieces facing and using long ends:

- Sew the base of Head to Body.
- Sew Arms to each side between Rnds 25 and 26 of Body.
- Sew Legs to each side across Rnds 7-10 of Body.
- Sew Ears to each side of Head, between Rnds 13 and 14.
- Sew Muzzle to front of Head across Rnds 5-9.
- Sew Nose to top of Muzzle across Rnds 4 and 5; add remaining feature using straight stitch ***(Fig. 14, page 62)***.
- Using satin stitch ***(Fig. 13a & b, page 62)***, add Black eyes across Rnds 11 and 12 of Head.
- Using straight stitch, add Lt Gray 'reflection' dot to each eye.

EASY

BUSTER

Mia always packs extra treats when she has to pick up Buster. He is a treat-hog. He will perform all the tricks, basically all at once just for that tasty treat! Shake, roll over, speak, sit...he has mastered them all.

GAUGE INFORMATION

8 sc and 9 rows = 2" (5 cm)
Gauge Swatch: 2" (5 cm) square
Ch 9.
Row 1: Sc in second ch from hook and in each ch across: 8 sc.
Rows 2-9: Ch 1, turn; sc in each sc across.
Finish off.

STITCH GUIDE

SINGLE CROCHET 2 TOGETHER *(abbreviated sc2tog)*
Pull up a loop in each of next 2 sts, YO and draw through all 3 loops on hook *(Fig. 8a, page 61)* **(counts as one sc)**.

BODY

Rnd 1 (Right side)**:** With Tan, make an adjustable loop to form a ring *(Figs. 5a-d, page 60)*, work 5 sc in ring; do **not** join, place marker to indicate the beginning of the rnd *(Fig. 1, page 60)*.

Note: Loop a short piece of yarn around any stitch to mark Rnd 1 as **right** side.

Rnd 2: 2 Sc in each sc around: 10 sc.

Rnd 3: (Sc in next sc, 2 sc in next sc) around: 15 sc.

Rnd 4: (Sc in next 2 sc, 2 sc in next sc) around: 20 sc.

Rnd 5: (Sc in next 3 sc, 2 sc in next sc) around: 25 sc.

Rnd 6: (Sc in next 4 sc, 2 sc in next sc) around: 30 sc.

Rnds 7-18: Sc in each sc around.

Rnd 19: (Sc in next 13 sc, sc2tog) twice: 28 sc.

Rnd 20: Sc in each sc around.

Rnd 21: (Sc in next 12 sc, sc2tog) twice: 26 sc.

Rnd 22: Sc in each sc around.

Rnd 23: (Sc in next 11 sc, sc2tog) twice: 24 sc.

Rnd 24: Sc in each sc around.

Finished Length:

Approx. 8" (20.5 cm)

Yarn (Medium Weight - 4)

7 ounces, 364 yards - per skein
(198 grams, 333 meters) - per skein
- ☐ Tan - 1 skein
- ☐ Brown - 1 skein
- ☐ White - xx yards (xx meters)
- ☐ Dk Gray - xx yards (xx meters)
- ☐ Green - small amount

Crochet Hook

☐ Size G (4 mm) **or** size needed for gauge

Additional Supplies

- ☐ Polyester fiberfill
- ☐ Yarn needle

Rnd 25: (Sc in next 10 sc, sc2tog) twice: 22 sc.

Rnd 26: Sc in each sc around.

Rnd 27: (Sc in next 9 sc, sc2tog) twice: 20 sc.

Rnd 28: (Sc in next 3 sc, sc2tog) around: 16 sc.

Rnd 29: (Sc in next 2 sc, sc2tog) around; slip st in next sc, finish off leaving an 8" (20.5 cm) length for sewing: 12 sts.

Stuff Body with polyester fiberfill.

Thread yarn needle with end and weave yarn thru Front Loops Only of remaining sc ***(Fig. 7, page 61)***; pull **tightly** to close hole and secure end.

HEAD

Rnd 1 (Right side)**:** With Tan, make an adjustable loop to form a ring, work 6 sc in ring; do **not** join, place marker to indicate the beginning of the rnd.

Note: Mark Rnd 1 as **right** side.

Rnd 2: 2 Sc in each sc around: 12 sc.

Rnd 3: (Sc in next sc, 2 sc in next sc) around: 18 sc.

Rnd 4: (Sc in next 2 sc, 2 sc in next sc) around: 24 sc.

Rnd 5: (Sc in next 3 sc, 2 sc in next sc) around: 30 sc.

Rnds 6-11: Sc in each sc around.

Rnd 12: (Sc in next 3 sc, sc2tog) around: 24 sc.

Rnd 13: (Sc in next 2 sc, sc2tog) around: 18 sc.

Rnd 14: (Sc in next sc, sc2tog) around: 12 sc.

Rnd 15: (Sc in next sc, sc2tog) around; slip st in next sc, finish off leaving an 8" (20.5 cm) length for sewing: 8 sts.

Stuff Head with polyester fiberfill.

Thread yarn needle with long end and weave needle thru Front Loops Only of remaining sc; pull **tightly** to close hole and secure end.

FRONT LEG (Make 2)

Rnd 1 (Right side)**:** With Brown, make an adjustable loop to form a ring, work 4 sc in ring; do **not** join, place marker to indicate the beginning of the rnd.

Note: Mark Rnd 1 as **right** side.

Rnd 2: 2 Sc in each sc around: 8 sc.

Rnd 3: (Sc in next sc, 2 sc in next sc) around: 12 sc.

Rnd 4: (Sc in next sc, sc2tog) around; slip st in next sc, finish off: 8 sts.

Rnd 5: With **right** side facing, join Tan with slip st in same st as joining ***(Fig. 2, page 60)***; ch 1, sc in same st and in each sc around; join with slip st to first sc.

Rnd 6: Ch 1, sc in same st as joining and in each sc around; do **not** join, place marker to indicate the beginning of the round.

Rnds 7 and 8: Sc in each sc around.

Rnd 9: (Sc2tog, sc in next 2 sc) twice: 6 sc.

Stuff Leg with polyester fiberfill.

Rnd 10: (Sc2tog, sc in next sc) twice; slip st in next sc, finish off leaving an 8" (20.5 cm) length for sewing: 4 sts.

BACK LEG (Make 2)

Work Rnds 1-8 of Front Leg: 8 sc.

Rnd 9: (Sc2tog, sc in next 2 sc) twice; slip st in next sc, finish off leaving an 8" (20.5 cm) length for sewing: 6 sts.

Stuff Leg with polyester fiberfill.

MUZZLE

Row 1 (Right side)**:** With White, ch 3, 2 sc in second ch from hook and in last ch: 4 sc.

Note: Mark Row 1 as **right** side.

Row 2: Ch 1, turn; 2 sc in first sc, sc in next 2 sc, 2 sc in last sc: 6 sc.

Row 3: Ch 1, turn; 2 sc in first sc, sc in next 4 sc, 2 sc in last sc: 8 sc.

Row 4: Ch 1, turn; sc in each sc across.

Row 5: Ch 1, turn; beginning in first sc, sc2tog, sc in next 4 sc, sc2tog: 6 sc.

Row 6: Ch 1, turn; beginning in first sc, sc2tog, sc in next 2 sc, sc2tog: 4 sc.

Row 7: Ch 1, turn; beginning in first sc, sc2tog twice; do **not** finish off: 2 sc.

TRIM

Rnd 1 (Right side)**:** Ch 1, do **not** turn; work 6 sc evenly spaced across end of rows; working in free loops of beginning ch ***(Fig. 9b, page 61)***, sc in next 2 chs; work 6 sc evenly spaced across end of rows; sc in each sc on Row 7; join with slip st to first sc: 16 sc.

Rnd 2: Ch 1, 2 sc in same st as joining, sc in next 3 sc, (2 sc in next sc, sc in next 3 sc) around; join with slip st to first sc, finish off leaving an 8" (20.5 cm) length for sewing: 20 sc.

EAR (Make 2)

Rnd 1 (Right side)**:** With Brown, make an adjustable loop to form a ring, work 3 sc in ring; do **not** join, place marker to indicate the beginning of the rnd.

Note: Mark Rnd 1 as **right** side.

Rnd 2: 2 Sc in each sc around: 6 sc.

Rnd 3: (Sc in next sc, 2 sc in next sc) around: 9 sc.

Rnd 4: (Sc in next 2 sc, 2 sc in next sc) around: 12 sc.

Rnd 5: (Sc in next 3 sc, 2 sc in next sc) around: 15 sc.

Rnds 6 and 7: Sc in each sc around.

Rnd 8: (Sc in next 3 sc, sc2tog) around: 12 sc.

Rnd 9: Sc in each sc around; slip st in next sc, finish off leaving a 6" (15 cm) length for sewing.

TAIL

Row 1 (Right side)**:** With Tan, ch 7, sc in second ch from hook and in ch each across: 6 sc.

Note: Mark Row 1 as **right** side.

Rows 2-4: Ch 1, turn; sc in each sc across; at end of Row 4, finish off leaving an 8" (20.5 cm) length for sewing.

With **wrong** side together, fold piece in half matching top of sc on Row 4 to free loops of beginning ch; sew seam, leaving remaining end for sewing.

COLLAR

Row 1 (Right side): With Green, ch 14; finish off leaving a 6" (15 cm) length for sewing.

Note: Mark Row 1 as **right** side.

FINISHING

Using photo as a guide for placement, with **right** sides of all pieces facing and using long ends:

- Sew Ears across Rnds 10-13 of Head.
- Sew Muzzle to Rnds 4 or 5 of Head.
- Using satin stitch ***(Fig. 13a & b, page 62)***, add Dk Gray nose to Muzzle; add eyes to Head across Rnd 6 having 5 sc between eyes.
- Using straight stitch ***(Fig. 14, page 62)***, add Dk Gray mouth.
- Using straight stitch, add White 'reflection' dot to each eye.
- Sew Head Rnds 8-11 across Rnds 24-27 of Body.
- Sew Front Legs to Body across Rnds 23-25.
- Sew Back Legs to Body across Rnds 7 and 8.
- Sew Tail to back of Body across Rnds 2 and 3.
- Place Collar around neck and sew ends of Collar together.

PAW RUG

After a quick walk around the park, Mia treats the dogs to a snack break at her house. There she has prepared a space with special handmade items. She loves her walking-companions and wants them to feel welcome in their home-away-from-home.

Mia took her time making nice accessories and decorated them with special touches. She really enjoyed making the big paw rug. She loves seeing the dogs snuggled up on it taking a break...and seeing Junior stretching from one side to the other!

Finished Size:

25½" (65 cm) diameter

Yarn
(Super Bulky Weight - 6)

3.5 ounces, 108 yards - per skein
(100 grams, 99 meters) - per skein

- ☐ Tan - 3 skeins
- ☐ Lt Brown - 3 skeins
- ☐ White - 1 skein **or** 20 yards (18.5 meters)

Crochet Hook

☐ Size K (6.5 mm) **or** size needed for gauge

Additional Supplies

☐ Yarn needle

GAUGE INFORMATION

Gauge Swatch:
5½" (14 cm) diameter
Work same as Rug through Rnd 3: 30 dc.

STITCH GUIDE

SINGLE CROCHET 2 TOGETHER ***(abbreviated sc2tog)***
Pull up a loop in each of next 2 sts, YO and draw through all 3 loops on hook ***(Fig. 8a, page 61)*** **(counts as one sc).**

SINGLE CROCHET 3 TOGETHER ***(abbreviated sc3tog)***
Pull up a loop in each of next 3 sts, YO and draw through all 4 loops on hook ***(Fig. 8d, page 61)*** **(counts as one sc).**

RUG

Rnd 1 (Right side)**:** With Tan, ch 3, 10 dc in third ch from hook; skip beginning ch and join with slip st to first dc: 10 dc.

Note: Loop a short piece of yarn around any stitch to mark Rnd 1 as **right** side.

Rnd 2: Ch 2 (does **not** count as a st, now and throughout), 2 dc in same st as joining and in each dc around; skip beginning ch and join with slip st to first dc: 20 dc.

Rnd 3: Ch 2, dc in same st as joining, 2 dc in next dc, (dc in next dc, 2 dc in next dc) around; skip beginning ch and join with slip st to first dc: 30 dc.

Rnd 4: Ch 2, dc in same st as joining and in next dc, 2 dc in next dc, (dc in next 2 dc, 2 dc in next dc) around; skip beginning ch and join with slip st to first dc: 40 dc.

Rnd 5: Ch 2, dc in same st as joining and in next 2 dc, 2 dc in next dc, (dc in next 3 dc, 2 dc in next dc) around; skip beginning ch and join with slip st to first dc: 50 dc.

Rnd 6: Ch 2, dc in first dc and in next 3 dc, 2 dc in next dc, (dc in next 4 dc, 2 dc in next dc) around; skip beginning ch and join with slip st to first dc: 60 dc.

Rnd 7: Ch 2, dc in same st as joining and in next 4 dc, 2 dc in next dc, (dc in next 5 dc, 2 dc in next dc) around; skip beginning ch and join with slip st to first dc: 70 dc.

Rnd 8: Ch 2, dc in same st as joining and in next 2 dc, 2 dc in next dc, (dc in next 6 dc, 2 dc in next dc) around, dc in last 3 dc; skip beginning ch and join with slip st to first dc: 80 dc.

Rnd 9: Ch 2, dc in first dc and in next 6 dc, 2 dc in next dc, (dc in next 7 dc, 2 dc in next dc) around; skip beginning ch and join with slip st to first dc: 90 dc.

Rnd 10: Ch 2, dc in same st as joining and in next 7 dc, 2 dc in next dc, (dc in next 8 dc, 2 dc in next dc) around; skip beginning ch and join with slip st to first dc: 100 dc.

Rnd 11: Ch 2, dc in same st as joining and in next 8 dc, 2 dc in next dc, (dc in next 9 dc, 2 dc in next dc) around; skip beginning ch and join with slip st to first dc: 110 dc.

Rnd 12: Ch 2, dc in same st as joining and in next 9 dc, 2 dc in next dc, (dc in next 10 dc, 2 dc in next dc) around; skip beginning ch and join with slip st to first dc: 120 dc.

Rnd 13: Ch 2, dc in same st as joining and in next 10 dc, (dc in next 11 dc, 2 dc in next dc) around; skip beginning ch and join with slip st to first dc: 130 dc.

Rnd 14: Ch 2, dc in same st as joining and in next 11 dc, (dc in next 12 dc, 2 dc in next dc) around; skip beginning ch and join with slip st to first dc: 140 dc.

Rnd 15: Ch 1, sc in same st as joining and in next 12 dc, 2 sc in next dc, (sc in next 13 dc, 2 sc in next dc) around; join with slip st to first sc, finish off: 150 sc.

Edging Rnd: With **right** side facing, join White with sc in same st as joining ***(Fig. 3, page 60)***; sc in next 13 sc, 2 sc in next sc, (sc in next 14 sc, 2 sc in next sc) around; join with slip st to first sc, finish off.

PAW PAD

With Lt Brown, ch 25.

Row 1 (Right side)**:** 2 Sc in second ch from hook, sc in each ch across to last sc, 2 sc in last sc: 26 sc.

Note: Mark Row 1 as **right** side.

Row 2: Ch 1, turn; 2 sc in first sc, sc in each sc across to last sc, 2 sc in last sc: 28 sc.

Row 3: Ch 1, turn; sc in each sc across.

Rows 4-6: Ch 1, turn; 2 sc in first sc, sc in each sc across to last sc, 2 sc in last sc: 34 sc.

Rows 7-16: Ch 1, turn; sc in each sc across.

Row 17 (Decrease row)**:** Ch 1, turn; beginning in first sc, sc2tog, sc in each sc across to last 2 sc, sc2tog: 32 sc.

Row 18 (Decrease row)**:** Ch 1, turn; beginning in first sc, sc3tog, sc in each sc across to last 3 sc, sc3tog: 28 sc.

Rows 19-21: Repeat Rows 17 and 18 once, then repeat Row 17 once **more**: 20 sc.

Row 22: Ch 1, turn; sc in each sc across.

Row 23: Ch 1, turn; beginning in first sc, sc2tog, sc in each sc across to last 2 sc, sc2tog: 18 sc.

Rows 24-27: Ch 1, turn; sc in each sc across.

Rows 28-30: Ch 1, turn; beginning in first sc, sc2tog, sc in each sc across to last 2 sc, sc2tog: 12 sc.

Edging Rnd: Ch 1, turn; beginning in first sc, sc2tog, sc in each sc across to last 2 sc, sc2tog; working in end of rows, skip Row 30, sc in each row across to beginning ch; working in free loops of beginning ch ***(Fig. 9b, page 61)***, sc in each ch across; working in end of rows, sc in each row across to Row 30, skip Row 30; join with slip st to first sc, finish off leaving a long end for sewing.

TOE PAD (Make 4)

Row 1 (Right side)**:** With Lt Brown, ch 4, 2 sc in second ch from hook, sc in next ch, 2 sc in last ch: 5 sc.

Note: Mark Row 1 as **right** side.

Row 2: Ch 1, turn; 2 sc in first sc, sc in next 3 sc, 2 sc in last sc: 7 sc.

Row 3: Ch 1, turn; sc in each sc across.

Rows 4 and 5: Ch 1, turn; 2 sc in first sc, sc in each sc across to last sc, 2 sc in last sc: 11 sc.

Rows 6-8: Ch 1, turn; sc in each sc across.

Rows 9 and 10: Ch 1, turn; beginning in first sc, sc2tog, sc in each sc across to last 2 sc, sc2tog: 7 sc.

Row 11: Ch 1, turn; sc in each sc across.

Row 12: Ch 1, turn; beginning in first sc, sc2tog, sc in next 3 sc, sc2tog: 5 sc.

Edging Rnd: Ch 1, turn; beginning in first sc, sc2tog, sc in next sc, sc2tog; working in end of rows, sc in each row across to beginning ch; working in free loops of beginning ch, sc in first 3 chs; working in end of rows, sc in each row across; join with slip st to first sc, finish off leaving a long end for sewing.

FINISHING

Using photo as a guide for placement and having **right** side of pieces facing, sew Paw Pad and Toes to **right** side of Rug.

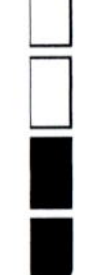

DOG BED

Dash always claims the dog bed. He should share, and he knows it, but he IS the biggest dog and needs it all to himself.

Finished Size:

(before assembly)
40" wide x 25½" tall
(101.5 cm x 64.5 cm)

Yarn

(Super Bulky Weight - 6)

35.2 ounces, 547 yards - per cake
(1,000 grams, 500 meters) - per cake
☐ 1 cake

Crochet Hook

☐ Size M/N (9 mm) **or** size needed for gauge

Additional Supplies

☐ Standard bed pillow
☐ Yarn needle

GAUGE INFORMATION

8 dc and 5 rows = 4" (10 cm)
Gauge Swatch: 4" (10 cm) square
Ch 10.
Row 1: Dc in fourth ch from hook **(3 skipped chs count as first dc)** and in each ch across: 8 dc.
Rows 2-5: Ch 3 **(counts as first dc)**, turn; dc in next dc and in each dc across.
Finish off.

PANEL

Ch 66.

Row 1 (Right side)**:** Sc in second ch from hook and in each ch across: 65 sc.

Note: Loop a short piece of yarn around any stitch to mark Row 1 as **right** side.

Row 2: Ch 2 (does **not** count as a st), turn; hdc in first sc, **[**pull up a loop in **next** sc (2 loops on hook), YO, pull up a loop in **next** sc, YO and draw through all 4 loops on hook **(counts as one st)]**, ★ ch 1, **[**pull up a loop in **next** sc (2 loops on hook), YO, pull up a loop in **next** sc, YO and draw through all 4 loops on hook **(counts as one st)]**; repeat from ★ across, hdc in turning ch: 66 sts.

Row 3: Ch 1, turn; skip first hdc, sc in next st, (sc in next ch-1 and in next st) across: 65 sc.

Rows 4-37: Repeat Rows 2 and 3, 17 times; do **not** finish off.

ASSEMBLY

With **right** side together, fold Panel in half having end of rows matching; working through **both** pieces, slip st across end of rows to beginning ch; matching free loops of beginning ch ***(Fig. 9b, page 61)***, slip st free loops together across to corner; finish off.

Turn piece **right** side out and insert bed pillow.

Matching sts on Row 37, join yarn with slip st through first sts; slip st through **both** loops of each st across to close opening; finish off.

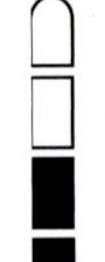

BONE PILLOW

Princess curls up by the bone pillow on the couch. She doesn't mind snuggling with Mia but won't let anyone else near her big bone!

GAUGE INFORMATION

With one strand of Color A and one strand of Color B held together,
7 sts and 7 rows = 4" (10 cm)
Gauge Swatch: 4" (10 cm) square
With one strand of Color A and one strand of Color B held together, ch 8.
Row 1: Sc in second ch from hook and in each ch across: 7 sc.
Rows 2-7: Ch 1, turn; sc in each sc across. Finish off.

STITCH GUIDE

SINGLE CROCHET 3 TOGETHER
(abbreviated sc3tog)
(uses next 3 sts)
Pull up a loop in next 3 sts indicated, YO and draw through all 4 loops on hook **(counts as one sc)**.

PANEL (Make 2)

With one strand of Color A and one strand of Color B held together, ch 26.

Row 1 (Right side)**:** Sc in second ch from hook and in each ch across: 25 sc.

Note: Loop a short piece of yarn around any stitch to mark Row 1 as **right** side.

Rows 2-12: Ch 1, turn; sc in each sc across.

Do **not** finish off.

ROUND ENDS OF BONE

PART 1
Row 1: Ch 3 **(counts as first dc)**, do **not** turn; 6 dc in last sc of Row 12, slip st in end of Row 10: 7 dc.

Note: Mark Row 1 as **right** side.

Row 2: Turn; 2 hdc in first dc and in each dc across; skip next 2 unworked sc on Row 12, slip st in next sc: 14 hdc.

Row 3: Slip st in next 2 sc on Row 12, turn; (2 dc in next hdc, dc in next hdc) across; slip st in end of Row 8, finish off: 21 dc.

PART 2
Row 1: With one strand of Color A and one strand of Color B held together, **right** side facing and working in free loops of beginning ch ***(Fig. 9b, page 61)***, join yarn with slip st in first ch ***(Fig. 2, page 60)***; ch 3 **(counts as first dc)**, 6 dc in same ch, skip next 2 unworked chs, slip st in next unworked ch: 7 dc.

Finished Size:

19" long x 13" high
(48.5 cm x 33 cm)

Yarn

(Super Bulky Weight - 6)

7 ounces, 188 yards - per skein
(200 grams, 172 meters) - per skein
☐ Color A - 1 skein

(Medium Weight - 4)

7 ounces, 359 yards - per skein
(200 grams, 328 meters) - per skein
☐ Color B - 1 skein

Crochet Hook

☐ Size M/N (9 mm) **or** size needed for gauge

Additional Supplies

☐ Polyester fiberfill
☐ Yarn needle

Row 2: Turn; 2 hdc in first dc and in each dc across; slip st in end of Row 4: 14 hdc.

Row 3: Slip st in end of Row 5, turn; (2 dc in next hdc, dc in next hdc) across, skip next unworked ch, slip st in next unworked ch, finish off.

PART 3

Row 1: With one strand of Color A and one strand of Color B held together, and **right** side facing, skip next 18 unworked chs, join yarn with slip st in next unworked ch; ch 3 **(counts as first dc)**, 6 dc in same ch, slip st in end of Row 4: 7 dc.

Row 2: Turn; 2 hdc in first dc and in each dc across, skip next 2 unworked chs, slip st in next unworked ch: 14 hdc.

Row 3: Slip st in next 2 unworked chs, turn; (2 dc in next hdc, dc in next hdc) across, slip st in end of Row 5, finish off.

PART 4

Row 1: With one strand of Color A and one strand of Color B held together, and **right** side facing, join yarn with slip st in first sc on Row 12; ch 3 **(counts as first dc)**, 6 dc in same st, skip next 2 unworked sc on Row 12, slip st in next unworked sc: 7 dc.

Row 2: Turn; 2 hdc in first dc and in each dc across, slip st to end of Row 9: 14 hdc.

Row 3: Slip st in next 2 end of Row 8, turn; (2 dc in next hdc, dc in next hdc) across, skip next unworked sc on Row 12, slip st to next unworked sc on Row 12; do **not** finish off.

TRIM

Rnd 1: Slip st in next 2 sts, ch 1, sc in same st and in next 10 sc, sc3tog using **next** sc, the **next** sc where Bone End joins and the **first** dc of Bone End, † 2 sc in next dc, (sc in next 2 dc, 2 sc in next dc) 6 times †, sc3tog using the **last** dc of Bone End, the **end** of Row 8 where Bone End joins and **end** of Row 7, sc3tog using **end** of Row 6, the **end** of Row 5 where Bone End joins and the **next** dc, repeat from † to † once, sc3tog using the **last** dc of Bone end, the **same** ch where Bone End joins and the **next** ch, sc in next 11 chs, sc3tog using the **next** ch, the **next** ch where Bone End joins and the **first** dc of Bone End, repeat from † to † once, sc3tog using **last** dc of Bone End, **end** of Row 5 where Bone End joins and the **end** of Row 6, sc3tog using **end** of Row 7, **end** of Row 8 where Bone End joins and the **first** dc of Bone End, repeat from † to † once, sc3tog using **last** dc of Bone End, the **same** sc where Bone End joins and the **first** slip st; join with slip st to first sc, finish off leaving a long length for sewing.

FINISHING

Thread yarn needle with long end of Medium Weight yarn from Trim. With **wrong** sides of **both** Panels together, sew Trim stitches together, stuffing piece firmly with polyester fiberfill before closing.

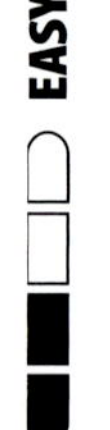

"HOUNDSTOOTH" FOOD MAT

Mia giggled while she crocheted the "houndstooth" food mat. She could imagine all the dogs eating their snacks. She loves that this mat is just for them! Plus, it keeps her floor clean…which is helpful with 8 slobbery dogs!

SIZE INFORMATION

Size Note: We have printed the instructions for the sizes in different colors to make it easier for you to find:

- size Small in Blue
- size Medium in Pink

Instructions in Black apply to all sizes.

GAUGE INFORMATION

Gauge: In pattern,
12½ sts and 12 rows = 4" (10 cm)

Gauge Swatch: 4½" x 4"
(11.5 cm x10 cm)

Ch 15.

Row 1: Sc in second ch from hook, dc in next ch, (sc in next ch, dc in next ch) across: 14 sc.

Rows 2-12: Ch 1, turn; sc in first dc, dc in next sc, (sc in next dc, dc in next sc) across.

Finish off.

BODY

With Gray, ch 31{41}.

Row 1 (Right side)**:** Sc in second ch from hook, dc in next ch, (sc in next ch, dc in next ch) across; finish off: 30{40} sts.

Note: Loop a short piece of yarn around any stitch to mark Row 1 as **right** side.

Row 2: With **wrong** side facing, join White with sc in first dc ***(Fig. 3, page 60)***; dc in next sc, (sc in next dc, dc in next sc) across; finish off.

Row 3: With **right** side facing, join Gray with sc in first dc; dc in next sc, (sc in next dc, dc in next sc) across; finish off.

Rows 4 thru 42{50}: Repeat Rows 2 and 3, 19{23} times; then repeat Row 2 once **more**.

Last Row: With **right** side facing, join Gray with sc in first dc; dc in next sc, (sc in next dc, dc in next sc) across; do **not** finish off.

TRIM

Rnd 1 (Right side)**:** Ch 1, do **not** turn; 2 sc in last dc made on Last Row, work 42{50} sc evenly spaced across end of rows to next corner; working in free loops of beginning ch ***(Fig. 9b, page 61)***, 3 sc in first ch, sc in next 28{38} chs, 3 sc in next ch; work 42{50} sc evenly space across end of rows to next corner; working in sts on Last Row, 3 sc in first sc, sc in next 28{38} sts, sc in same st as first sc; join with slip st to first sc: 152{188} sc.

Rnd 2: Ch 1, sc in same st as joining and in next 44{52} sc, 2 sc in next sc, sc in next 30{40} sc, 2 sc in next sc, sc in next 44{52} sc, 2 sc in next sc, sc in next 30{40} sc **and** in same st as first sc; join with slip st to first sc; finish off.

Finished Size:

Small
15" wide x 10½" high
(38 cm x 26.5 cm)

Medium
18½" wide x 13¾" high
(47 cm x 35 cm)

Yarn
(Medium Weight - 4)

1.75 ounces, 80 yards - per skein
(50 grams, 73 meters) - per skein

☐ Gray - 1{2} skein(s)
☐ White - 1{2} skein(s)

Crochet Hook

☐ Size G (4 mm) **or** size needed for gauge

Additional Supplies

☐ Yarn needle

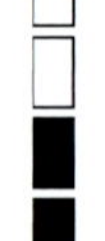

TOY BASKET

After a quick rest, the dogs have a jolt of energy, and they pull out the toy basket. Good thing Mia made a cute and durable basket to keep track of all of the toys. They do end up everywhere, but the dogs know where to find them every day…in the basket!

Finished Size:

10" circumference x 8" high (25.5 cm x 20.5 cm)

Yarn
(Super Bulky Weight - 6)

3.5 ounces, 55 yards - per skein (100 grams, 50 meters) - per skein

☐ Lt Grey - 2 skeins
☐ Lt Green - 1 skein (wind into 2 equal size balls)

Crochet Hook

☐ Size K (6.5 mm) **or** size needed for gauge

GAUGE INFORMATION

Gauge Swatch: 3" (7.5 cm) diameter
Work same as Bottom through Rnd 2: 20 sc.

STITCH GUIDE

SINGLE CROCHET 2 TOGETHER ***(abbreviated sc2tog)***
Pull up a loop in Front Loop Only of each of next 2 sc ***(Fig. 7, page 61)***, YO and draw through all 3 loops on hook ***(Fig. 8a, page 61)*** **(counts as one sc)**.

BOTTOM

Rnd 1 (Right side)**:** With 2 strands of Lt Grey held together, ch 3; work 10 dc in third ch from hook; join with slip st to first dc: 10 dc.

Note: Loop a short piece of yarn around any stitch to mark Rnd 1 as **right** side.

Rnd 2: Ch 1, 2 sc in same st as joining and in each dc around; join with slip st to first sc: 20 sc.

Rnd 3: Ch 2 (does **not** count as a st), dc in same st as joining, 2 dc in next sc, (dc in next sc, 2 dc in next sc) around; join with slip st to first dc: 30 dc.

Rnd 4: Ch 1, sc in same st as joining and in next dc, 2 sc in next dc, (sc in next 2 dc, 2 sc in next dc) around; join with slip st to first sc: 40 sc.

Rnd 5: Ch 2, dc in same st as joining and in next 2 sc, 2 dc in next sc, (dc in next 3 sc, 2 dc in next sc) around; join with slip st to first dc: 50 dc.

Rnd 6: Ch 1, sc in same st as joining and in next 3 dc, 2 sc in next dc, (sc in next 4 dc, 2 sc in next dc) around; join with slip st to first sc: 60 sc.

Rnd 7: Ch 2, dc in same st as joining and in next 4 sc, 2 dc in next sc, (dc in next 5 sc, 2 dc in next dc) around; join with slip st to first sc, do **not** finish off: 70 dc.

SIDES

Rnd 1: Ch 1, working in Back Loops Only *(Fig. 7, page 61)*, sc in same st as joining and in each dc around; join with slip st to **both** loops of first sc.

Rnd 2: Ch 1, sc in same st as joining and in each sc around; do **not** join, place marker to indicate the beginning of the rnd *(Fig. 1, page 60)*.

Rnds 3-13: Sc in each sc around; at end of Rnd 13, slip st in next sc, finish off.

Rnd 14: With 2 strands of Lt Green held together and **right** side facing, join Lt Green with sc in same st as slip st *(Fig. 3, page 60)*; sc in each sc around; join with slip st to first sc.

Rnds 15 and 16: Ch 1, sc in same st as joining and in each sc around; join with slip st to first sc.

Rnd 17: Ch 1, sc in same st as joining and in next 4 sc, sc2tog, (sc in next 5 sc, sc2tog) around; join with slip st to first sc: 60 sc.

Rnd 18: Ch 1, sc in same st and in next 4 sc, dc in next sc, ch 7, skip next 7 sc (**first handle**), dc in next sc, sc in next 21 sc, dc in next sc, ch 7, skip next 7 sc (**second handle**), dc in next sc, sc in next 16 sc; join with slip st to first sc: 46 sts and 2 ch-7 sps.

Rnd 19: Ch 1, sc in same st as joining and in next 5 sts, 7 sc in next ch-7 sp, sc in next 23 sts, 7 sc in next ch-7 sp, sc in last 17 sts; join with slip st to first sc, finish off.

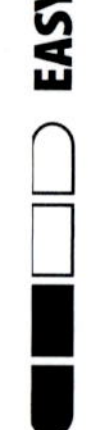

PUPPY LOVE BLANKET

After a long day, Mia returns each dog to their owner and heads home to relax. She picks up her crochet hook and kicks back. Her hook and yarn dance to the sounds of her favorite show and a blanket slowly begins to form. Mia loves her job and has decided that this blanket will be embellished with a bone appliqué to pay tribute to her doggy pack.

And now it's time to get some rest…because those dogs won't walk themselves! Tomorrow brings a new day, new sniffs and new treats.

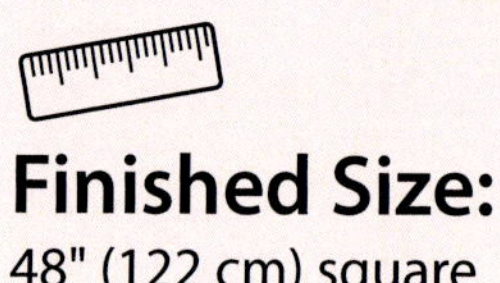

Finished Size:

48" (122 cm) square

Yarn (Medium Weight - 4)

5 ounces, 256 yards - per skein
(141 grams, 234 meters) - per skein

- ☐ Blue - 3 skeins
- ☐ Brown - 3 skeins
- ☐ Off White - 2 skeins

Crochet Hook

☐ Size J (6 mm) **or** size needed for gauge

GAUGE INFORMATION

Gauge Swatch: 4" (10 cm) square
Work same as Body thru Rnd 3: 36 dc and 4 corner ch-1 sps.

STITCH GUIDE

TREBLE CROCHET *(abbreviated tr)*
YO twice, insert hook in st indicated, YO and pull up a loop (4 loops on hook), (YO and draw through 2 loops on hook) 3 times ***(Figs. 19a-c, page 63)***.

BODY

With Blue, ch 4; join with slip st to form a ring.

Rnd 1 (Right side)**:** Ch 3 **(counts as first dc, now and throughout)**, 2 dc in ring, ch 1, (3 dc in ring, ch 1) 3 times; join with slip st to first dc: 12 dc and 4 ch-1 sps.

Note: Loop a short piece of yarn around any stitch to mark Rnd 1 as **right** side.

Rnd 2: Slip st in next 2 dc and in next ch-1 sp, ch 3, (2 dc, ch 1, 3 dc) in same sp **(corner made)**, skip next 3 dc, ★ (3 dc, ch 1, 3 dc) in next ch-1 sp **(corner made)**, skip next 3 sts; repeat from ★ 2 times **more**; join with slip st to first dc: 24 dc and 4 corner ch-1 sps.

Rnd 3: Slip st in next 2 dc and in next corner ch-1 sp, ch 3, (2 dc, ch 1, 3 dc) in same corner sp, ★ skip next 3 dc, 3 dc in sp **before** next dc ***(Fig. 11, page 62)***, skip next 3 dc, (3 dc, ch 1, 3 dc) in next corner ch-1 sp; repeat from ★ 2 times **more**, skip next 3 dc, 3 dc in sp **before** next dc, skip next 3 sts; join with slip st to first dc, finish off: 36 dc and 4 corner ch-1 sps.

Rnd 4: With **right** side facing, join Brown with dc in any corner ch-1 sp ***(Fig. 4, page 60)***; (2 dc, ch 1, 3 dc) in same corner sp, ★ † skip next 3 dc, (3 dc in sp **before** next dc, skip next 3 dc) across to next corner ch-1 sp †, (3 dc, ch 1, 3 dc) in corner sp; repeat from ★ 2 times **more**, then repeat from † to † once; join with slip st to first dc: 48 dc and 4 corner ch-1 sps.

Rnd 5: Slip st in next 2 dc and in next corner ch-1 sp, ch 3, (2 dc, ch 1, 3 dc) in same corner sp, ★ † skip next 3 dc, (3 dc in sp **before** next dc, skip next 3 dc) across to next corner ch-1 sp †, (3 dc, ch 1, 3 dc) in corner sp; repeat from ★ 2 times **more**, then repeat from † to † once; join with slip st to first dc: 60 dc and 4 corner ch-1 sps.

Rnd 6: Slip st in next 2 dc and in next corner ch-1 sp, ch 3, (2 dc, ch 1, 3 dc) in same corner sp, ★ † skip next 3 dc, (3 dc in sp **before** next dc, skip next 3 dc) across to next corner ch-1 sp †, (3 dc, ch 1, 3 dc) in corner sp; repeat from ★ 2 times **more**, then repeat from † to † once; join with slip st to first dc, finish off: 72 dc and 4 corner ch-1 sps.

Rnds 7-9: With Off White, repeat Rnds 4-6: 108 dc and 4 corner ch-1 sps.

Rnds 10-12: With Blue, repeat Rnds 4-6: 144 dc and 4 corner ch-1 sps.

Rnds 13-39: Repeat Rows 4-12, 3 times: 468 and 4 corner ch-1 sps.

Rnd 40: With **right** side facing, join Brown with dc in any corner ch-1 sp; (2 dc, ch 1, 3 dc) in same corner sp, ★ † dc in next 3 dc, (dc in sp **before** next dc, dc in next 3 dc) across to next corner ch-1 sp †, (3 dc, ch 1, 3 dc) in corner sp; repeat from ★ 2 times **more**, then repeat from † to † once; join with slip st to first dc, finish off: 644 dc and 4 corner ch-1 sps.

Edging Rnd: With **right** side facing, join Off White with slip st in any corner ch-1 sp; ch 1, working from **left** to **right**, work reverse sc in each dc around, working 3 reverse sc in each corner ch-1 sp; join with slip st to first st, finish off.

REVERSE SINGLE CROCHET

(abbreviated reverse sc)

Working from **left** to **right**, ★ insert hook in st to **right** of hook ***(Fig. A)***, YO and draw through, under and to **left** of loop on hook (2 loops on hook) ***(Fig. B)***, YO and draw through both loops on hook ***(Fig. C)*** **(reverse sc made, *Fig. D*)**; repeat from ★ around.

Fig. A

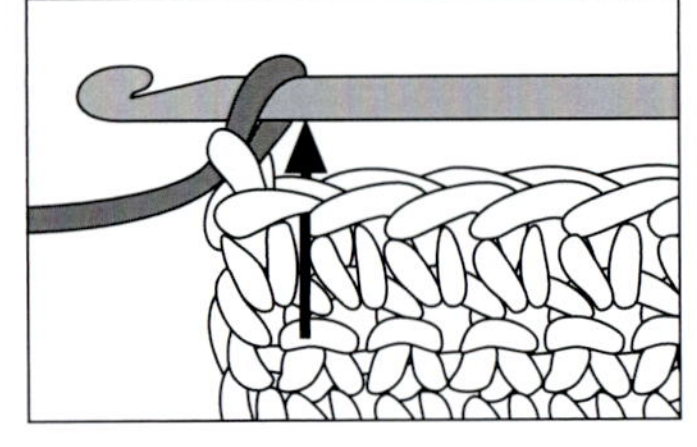

Fig. B

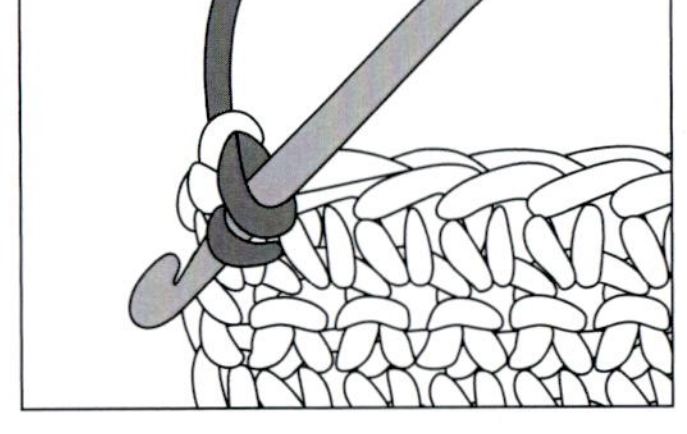

Fig. C

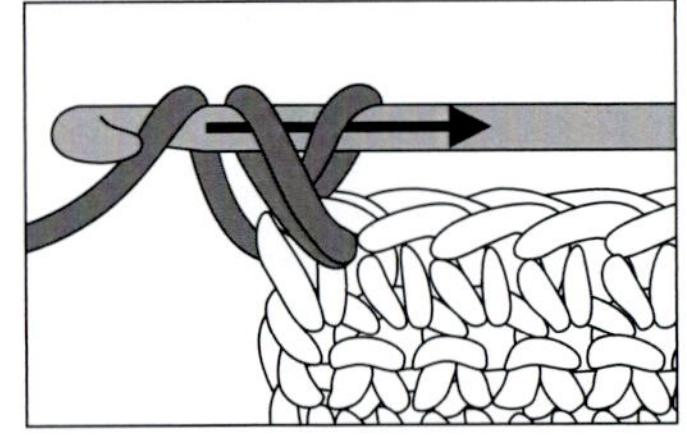

Fig. D

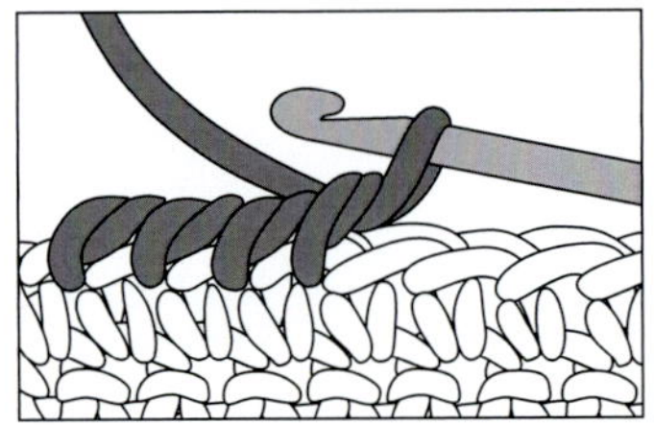

BONE APPLIQUÉ

With Off White, ch 21.

Rnd 1 (Right side)**:** Dc in third ch from hook and in each ch across to last ch, 5 dc in last ch; working in free loops of beginning ch ***(Fig. 9b, page 61)***, dc in next 17 chs, 4 dc in next ch; skip top of beginning ch and join with slip st to first dc: 44 dc.

Note: Mark Rnd 1 as **right** side.

Rnd 2: Ch 2 (does **not** count as a st), dc in same st as joining and in next 18 dc, 3 dc in next dc, dc in next dc, 3 dc in next dc, dc in next 19 dc, 3 dc in next dc, dc in next dc, 3 dc in next dc; join with slip st to first dc: 52 dc.

Rnd 3: Slip st in next 2 dc, ch 1, sc in same dc and in next 14 dc, † skip next 2 dc, (dc, 7 tr, dc) in next dc, skip next 2 dc, sc in next dc, skip next 2 dc, (dc, 7 tr, dc) in next dc, skip next 2 sts †, sc in next 15 dc, repeat from † to †once; join with slip st to first sc: 68 sts.

Rnd 4: Slip st in next 14 sc, † dc in next dc, 2 dc in each of next 3 tr, 3 dc in next tr, 2 dc in each of next 3 tr, dc in next dc †, slip st in next 15 sc, repeat from † to † once; join with slip st to first slip st.

Finish off leaving a long end for sewing.

Using photo as a guide for placement, sew Bone on corner of Blanket.

GENERAL INSTRUCTIONS

ABBREVIATIONS

ch(s)	chain(s)
cm	centimeters
dc	double crochet(s)
dc2tog	double crochet 2 together
dc3tog	double crochet 3 together
hdc	half double crochet(s)
hdc2tog	half double crochet 2 together
in.	inch(es)
Rnd(s)	Round(s)
sc	single crochet(s)
sc2tog	single crochet 2 together
sc3tog	single crochet 3 together
sp(s)	space(s)
st(s)	stitch(es)
tr	treble crochet(s)
YO	yarn over

SYMBOLS & TERMS

★ — work instructions following ★ as many **more** times as indicated in addition to the first time.

† to † — work all instructions from first † to second † **as many** times as specified.

( ) or [ ] — work enclosed instructions **as many** times as specified by the number immediately following **or** contains explanatory remarks.

colon (:) — the number(s) given after a colon at the end of a row or round denote(s) the number of stitches you should have on that row or round.

GAUGE

Exact gauge is essential for proper size. Before beginning your project, make the sample swatch given in the instructions in the yarn and hook specified. After completing the swatch, measure it, counting your stitches and rows or rounds carefully. If your swatch is larger or smaller than specified, **make another, changing hook size to get the correct gauge**. Keep trying until you find the size hook that will give you the specified gauge.

CROCHET TERMINOLOGY		
UNITED STATES		INTERNATIONAL
slip stitch (slip st)	=	single crochet (sc)
single crochet (sc)	=	double crochet (dc)
half double crochet (hdc)	=	half treble crochet (htr)
double crochet (dc)	=	treble crochet (tr)
treble crochet (tr)	=	double treble crochet (dtr)
double treble crochet (dtr)	=	triple treble crochet (ttr)
triple treble crochet (tr tr)	=	quadruple treble crochet (qtr)
skip	=	miss

Yarn Weight Symbol & Names	LACE 0	SUPER FINE 1	FINE 2	LIGHT 3	MEDIUM 4	BULKY 5	SUPER BULKY 6	JUMBO 7
Type of Yarns in Category	Fingering, size 10 crochet thread	Sock, Fingering, Baby	Sport, Baby	DK, Light Worsted	Worsted, Afghan, Aran	Chunky, Craft, Rug	Super Bulky, Roving	Jumbo, Roving
Crochet Gauge* Ranges in Single Crochet to 4" (10 cm)	32-42 sts**	21-32 sts	16-20 sts	12-17 sts	11-14 sts	8-11 sts	6-9 sts	5 sts and fewer
Advised Hook Size Range	Steel*** 6 to 8, Regular hook B-1	B-1 to E-4	E-4 to 7	7 to I-9	I-9 to K-10½	K-10½ to M/N-13	M/N-13 to Q	Q and larger

*GUIDELINES ONLY: The chart above reflects the most commonly used gauges and hook sizes for specific yarn categories.

BASIC	Projects using basic stitches. May include basic increases and decreases.
EASY	Projects may include simple stitch patterns, color work, and/or shaping.
INTERMEDIATE	Projects may include involved stitch patterns, color work, and/or shaping.
COMPLEX	Projects may include complex stitch patterns, color work, and/or shaping using a variety of techniques and stitches simultaneously.

CROCHET HOOKS																	
U.S.	B-1	C-2	D-3	E-4	F-5	G-6	7	H-8	I-9	J-10	K-10½	L-11	M/N-13	N/P-15	P/Q	Q	S
Metric - mm	2.25	2.75	3.25	3.5	3.75	4	4.5	5	5.5	6	6.5	8	9	10	15	16	19

MARKERS

Markers are used to help distinguish the beginning of each round being worked. Place a 2" (5 cm) scrap piece of yarn before the first stitch of each round ***(Fig. 1)***, moving marker after each round is complete.

Fig. 1

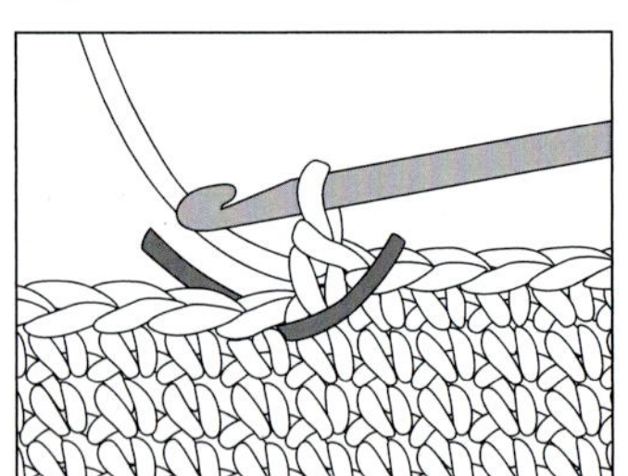

JOINING WITH A SLIP ST

When instructed to join with a slip st, begin with a slip knot on hook. Insert hook in st or sp indicated, YO and draw through st or sp and through loop on hook ***(Fig. 2)***.

Fig. 2

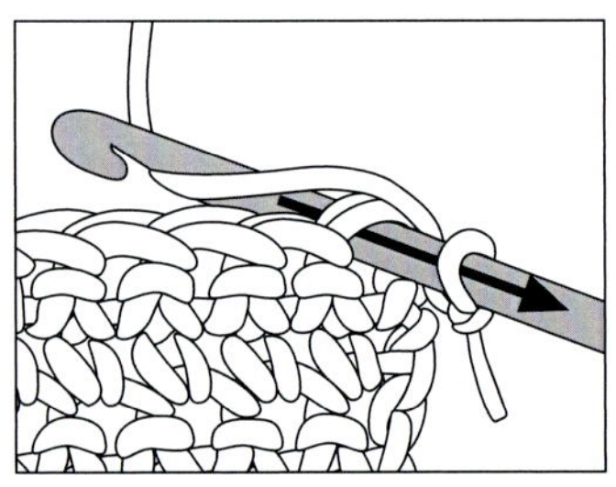

JOINING WITH A SC

When instructed to join with a sc, begin with a slip knot on hook. Insert hook in stitch or space indicated, YO and pull up a loop, YO and draw through both loops on hook ***(Fig. 3)***.

Fig. 3

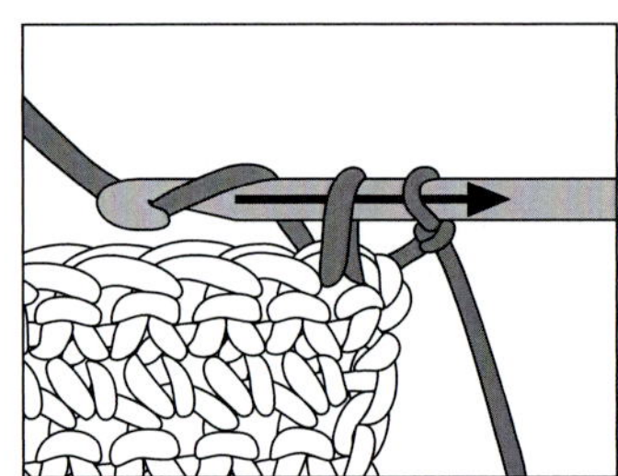

JOINING WITH A DC

When instructed to join with a dc, begin with a slip knot on hook. YO, holding loop on hook, insert hook in stitch or space indicated, YO and pull up a loop (3 loops on hook), (YO and draw through 2 loops on hook) twice ***(Fig. 4)***.

Fig. 4

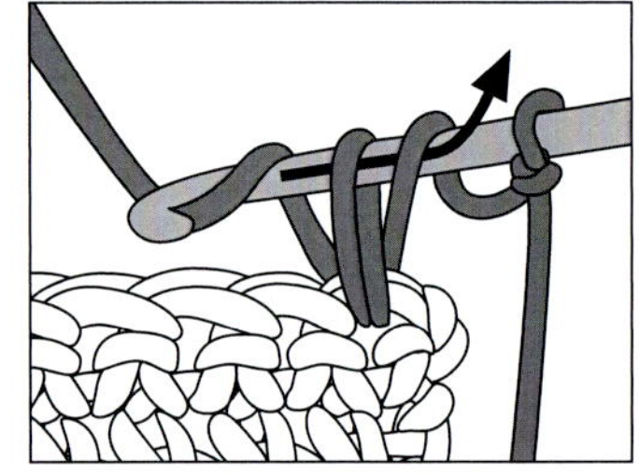

ADJUSTABLE LOOP

Wind yarn around two fingers to form a ring ***(Fig. 5a)***.

Fig. 5a

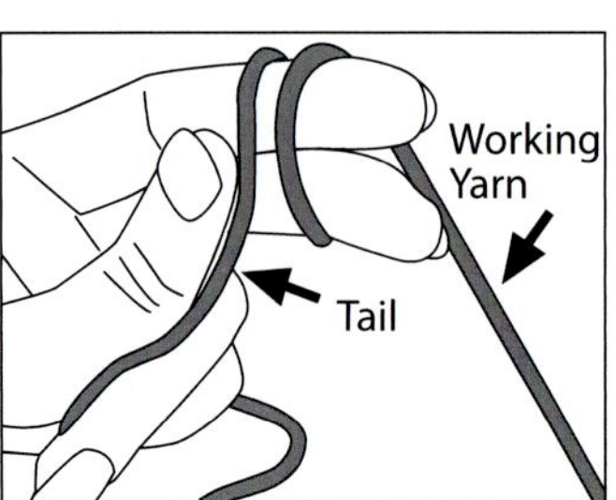

Slide yarn off fingers and grasp the strands at the top of the ring ***(Fig. 5b)***.

Fig. 5b

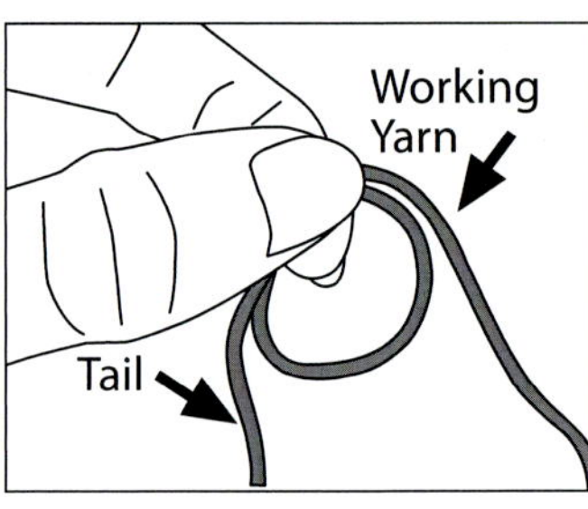

Insert hook from **front** to **back** into the ring, pull up a loop, YO and draw through loop on hook to lock ring ***(Fig. 5c)*** **(st made does not count as part of beginning ch of first rnd)**.

Fig. 5c

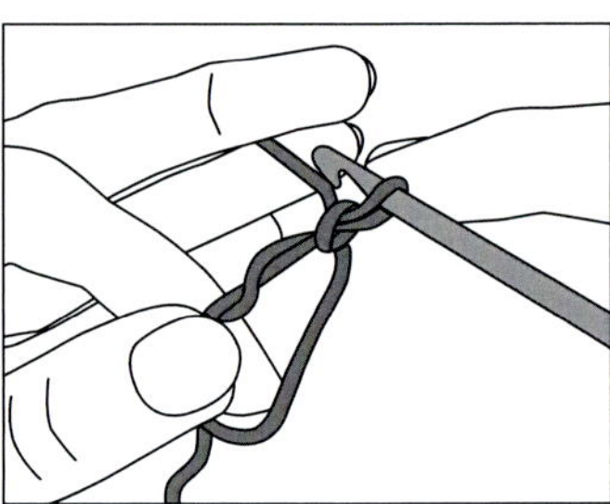

Working around both strands, follow instructions to work sts in the ring, then pull yarn tail to close ***(Fig. 5d)***.

Fig. 5d

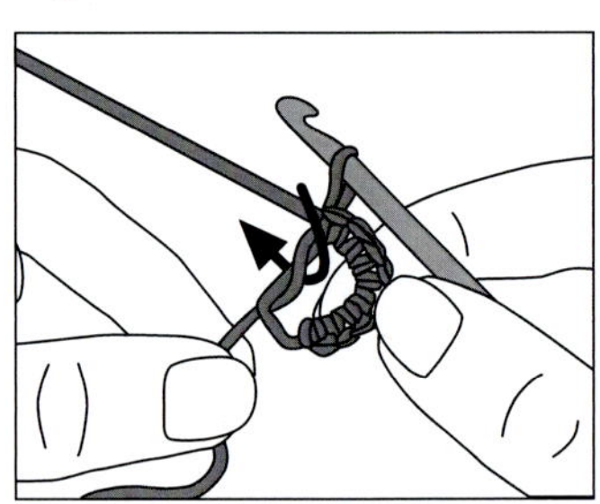

BACK RIDGE OF A CHAIN

Work in loops indicated by arrows *(Fig. 6)*.

Fig. 6

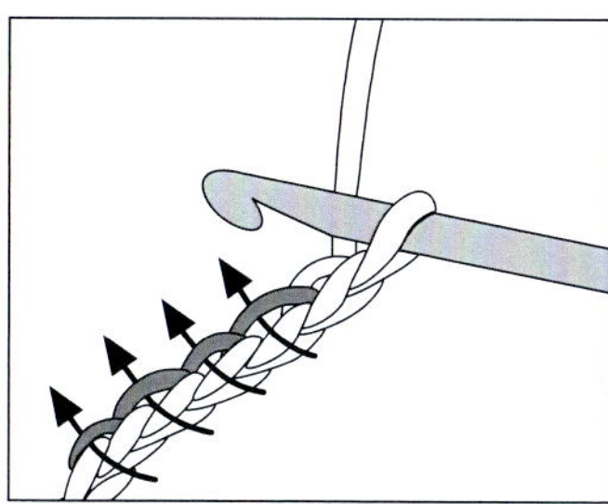

BACK OR FRONT LOOPS ONLY

Work only in loop(s) indicated by arrow *(Fig. 7)*.

Fig. 7

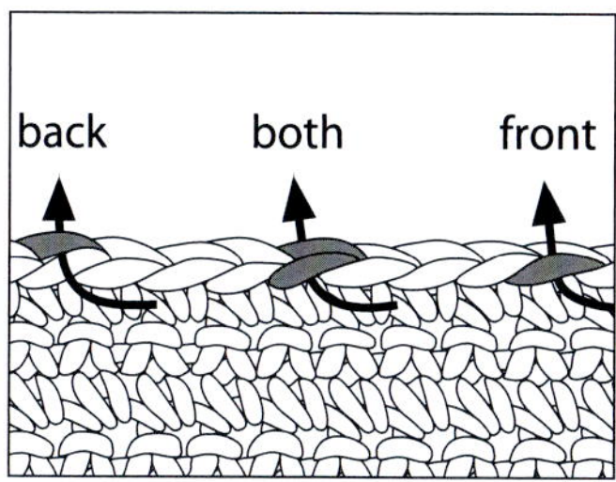

DECREASES

Single Crochet 2 Together

(abbreviated sc2tog)

Pull up a loop in each of next 2 sts, YO and draw through all 3 loops on hook ***(Fig. 8a)*** **(counts as one sc)**.

Fig. 8a

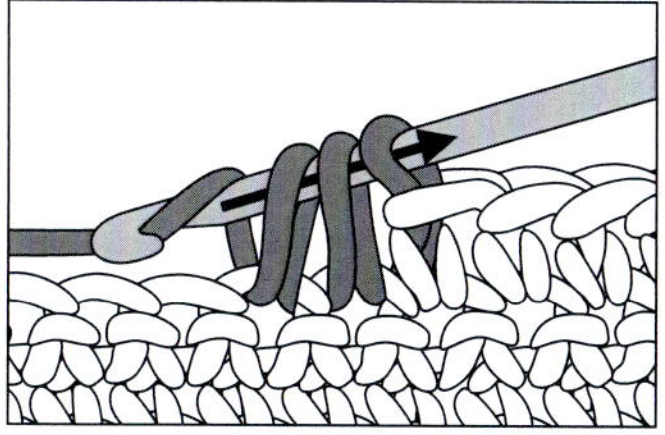

Half Double Crochet 2 Together

(abbreviated hdc2tog)

(uses next 2 sts)

★ YO, insert hook in **next** st, YO and pull up a loop; repeat from ★ once **more**, YO and draw through all 5 loops on hook ***(Fig. 8b)*** **(counts as one hdc)**.

Fig. 8b

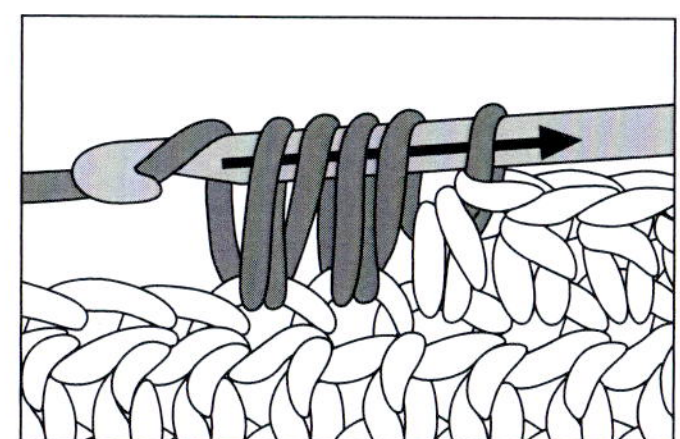

Double Crochet 2 Together

(abbreviated dc2tog)

(uses next 2 sts)

★ YO, insert hook in **next** st, YO and pull up a loop, YO and draw through 2 loops on hook; repeat from ★ once **more**, YO and draw through all 3 loops on hook ***(Fig. 8c)***.

Fig. 8c

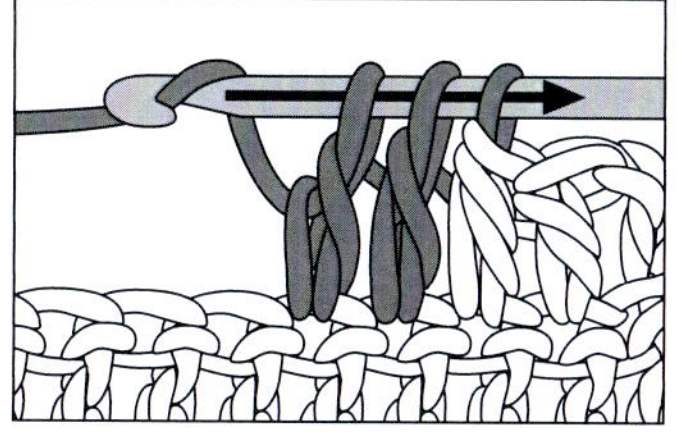

Single Crochet 3 Together

(abbreviated sc3tog)

Pull up a loop in each of next 3 sts, YO and draw through all 4 loops on hook ***(Fig. 8d)*** **(counts as one sc)**.

Fig. 8d

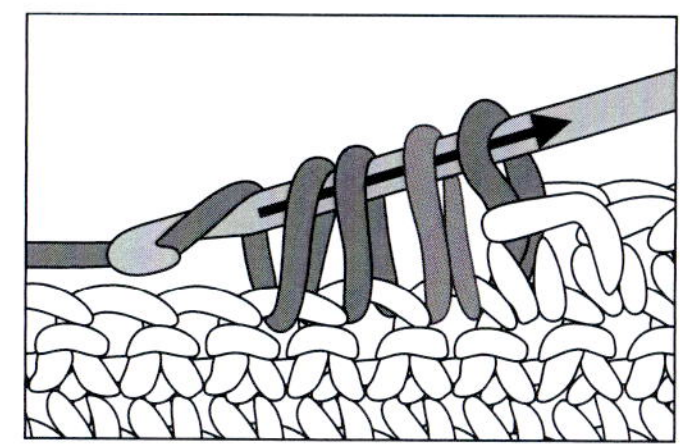

FREE LOOPS

After working in Back or Front Loops Only on a row or round, there will be a ridge of unused loops. These are called the free loops. Later, when instructed to work in the free loops of the same row or round, work in these loops ***(Fig. 9a)***.

Fig. 9a

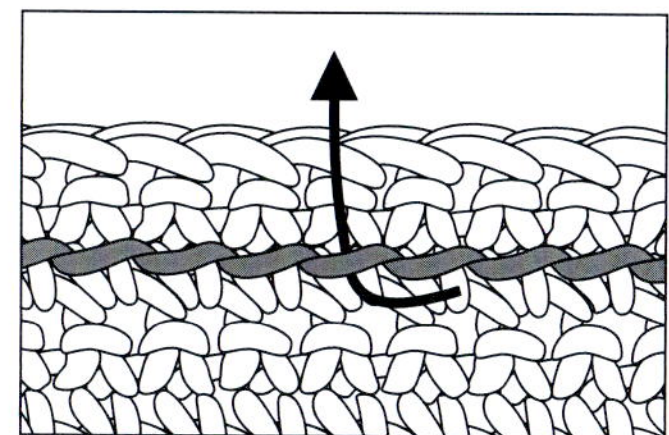

When instructed to work in free loops of a chain, work in loop indicated by arrow ***(Fig. 9b)***.

Fig. 9b

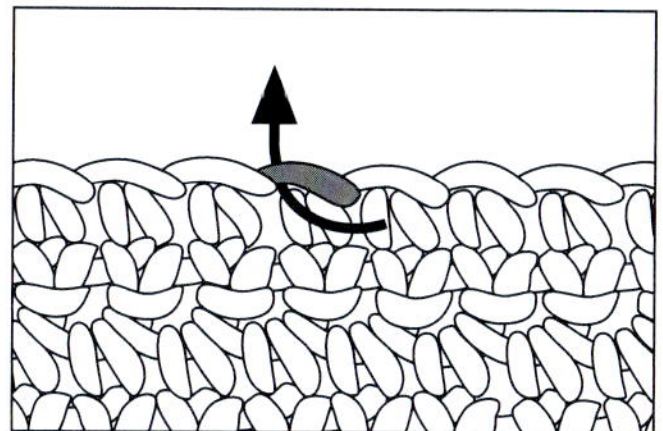

CHANGING COLORS

Work the last stitch to within one step of completion, hook new yarn ***(Fig. 10)*** and draw through both loops on hook. Cut old yarn and work over both ends.

Fig. 10

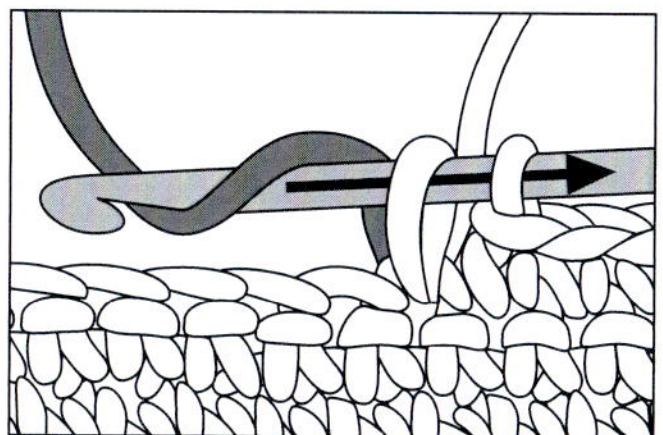

WORKING IN A SPACE BEFORE A STITCH

When instructed to work in a space **before** a stitch or in spaces **between** stitches, insert hook in space indicated by arrow ***(Fig. 11)***.

Fig. 11

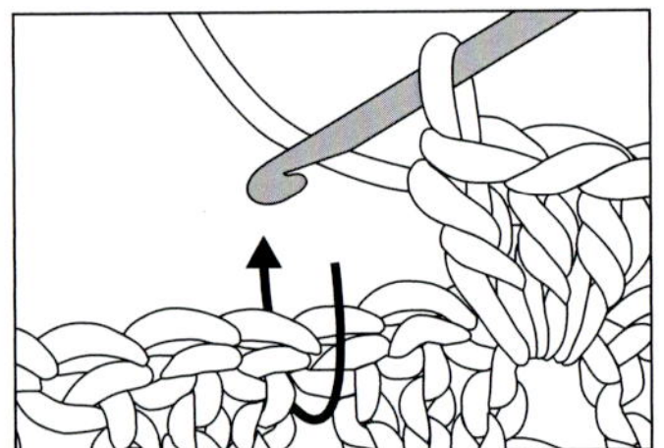

WEAVE THRU STITCHES

Weave yarn end through the stitches ***(Fig. 12)*** and gather to close.

Fig. 12

EMBROIDERY STITCHES

Satin Stitch

Satin stitch is a series of straight stitches entering and exiting the same hole. Bring the needle up at 1 and go down at 2 ***(Fig. 13a)***.

Fig. 13a

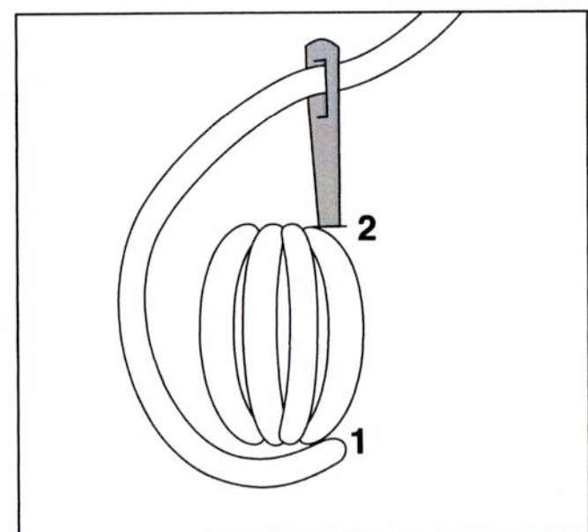

Satin stitch is also a series of straight stitches worked side-by-side, so they touch but do not overlap. Come up at odd numbers and go down at even numbers ***(Fig. 13b)***.

Fig. 13b

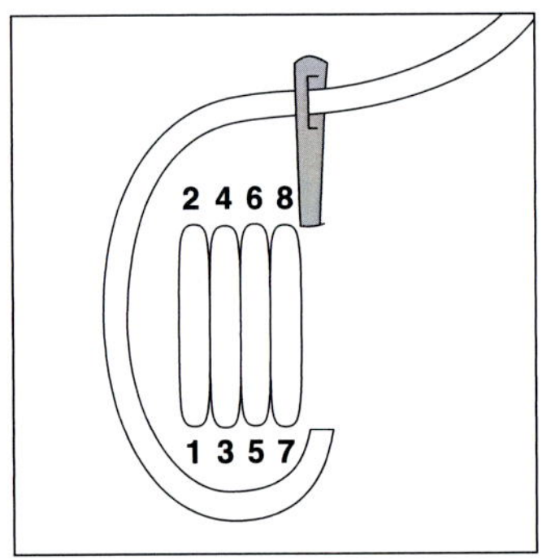

Straight Stitch

Straight stitch is just what the name implies, a single, straight stitch. Come up at 1 and go down at 2 ***(Fig. 14)***.

Fig. 14

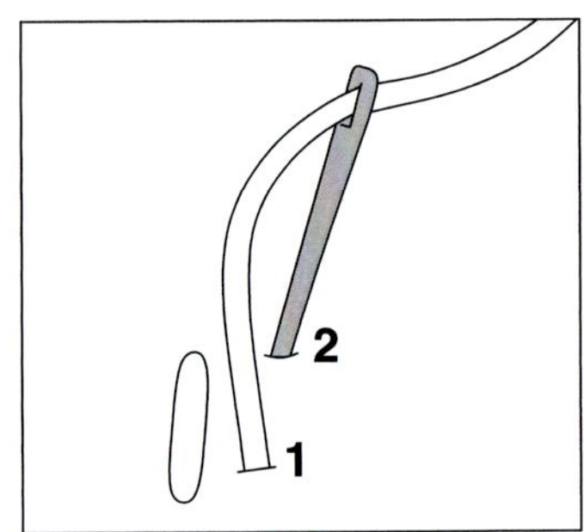

BASIC CROCHET STITCHES

SLIP STITCH

Insert hook in stitch indicated, YO and draw through st and through loop on hook ***(Fig.15)*** ***(abbreviated slip st)***.

Fig. 15

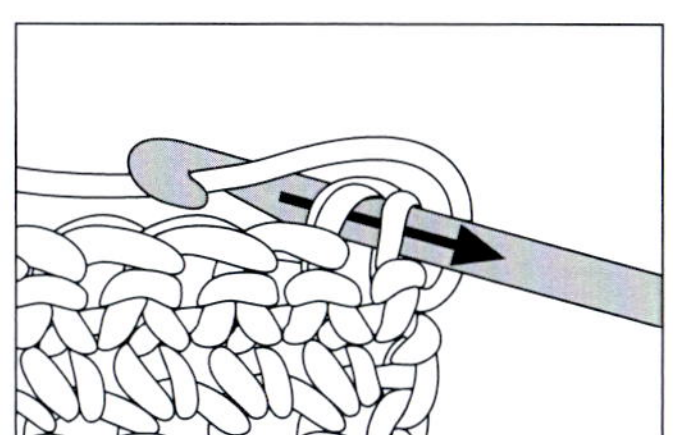

SINGLE CROCHET

Insert hook in stitch indicated, YO and pull up a loop, YO and draw through both loops on hook ***(Fig. 16)*** ***(abbreviated sc)***.

Fig. 16

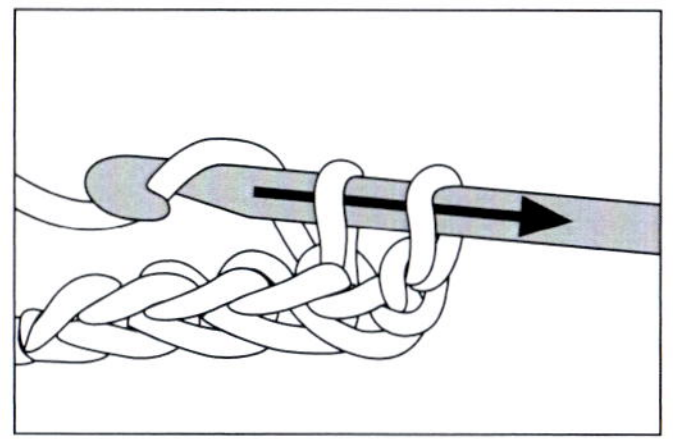

HALF DOUBLE CROCHET

YO, insert hook in stitch indicated, YO and pull up a loop, YO and draw through all 3 loops on hook ***(Fig. 17)*** ***(abbreviated hdc)***.

Fig. 17

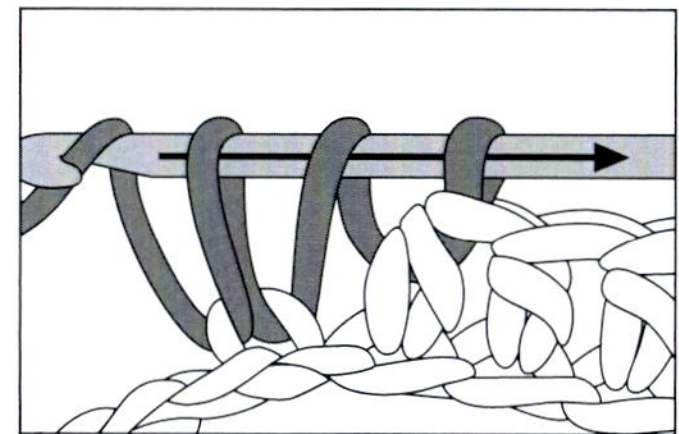

DOUBLE CROCHET

YO, insert hook in stitch indicated, YO and pull up a loop (3 loops on hook), YO and draw through 2 loops on hook ***(Fig. 18a)***, YO and draw through remaining 2 loops on hook ***(Fig. 18b)*** ***(abbreviated dc)***.

Fig. 18a

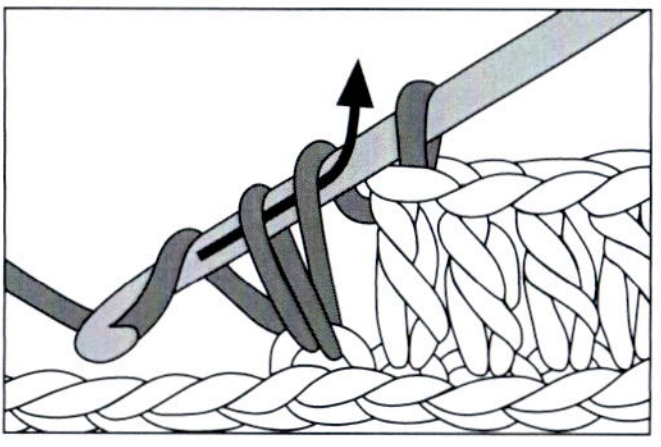

Fig. 18b

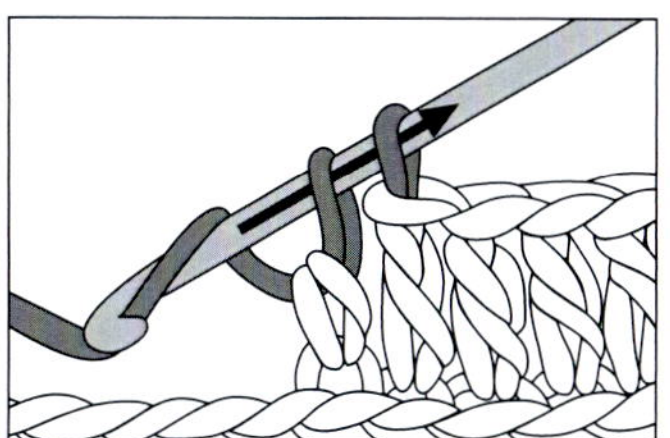

TREBLE CROCHET

YO twice, insert hook in stitch indicated, YO and pull up a loop (4 loops on hook) ***(Fig. 19a)***, (YO and draw through 2 loops on hook) 3 times ***(Fig. 19b & c)*** ***(abbreviated tr)***.

Fig. 19a

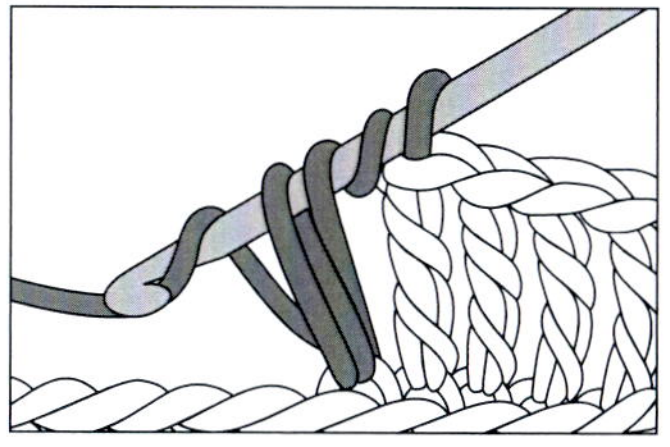

Fig. 19b

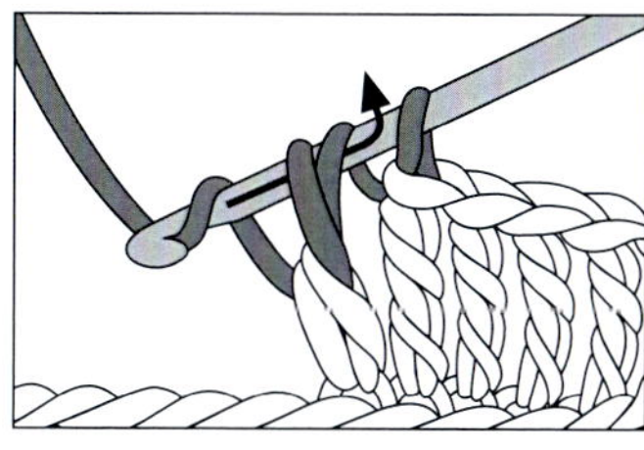

Fig. 19c

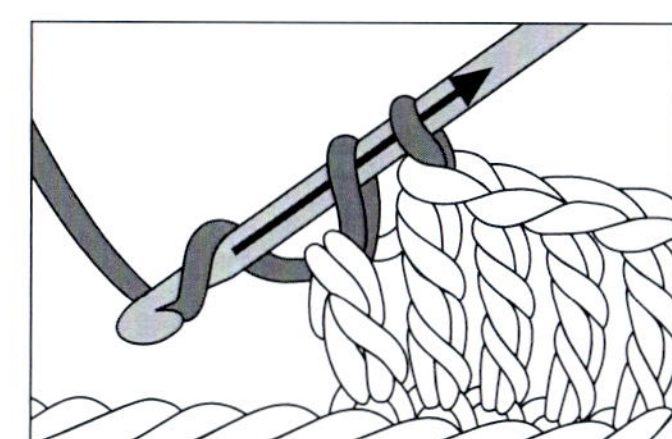

YARN INFORMATION

The projects in this book were made using a variety of yarn weights. Any brand of the specified yarn weight may be used. It is best to refer to the yardage/meters when determining how many ball or skeins to purchase. Remember, to arrive at the finished size, it is the GAUGE/TENSION that is important, not the brand of yarn.

For your convenience, listed below are the specific brands and yarn colors used to create our photography models. Because manufacturers make frequent changes in their product lines, you may sometimes find it necessary to use a substitute yarn or search for the discontinued product at alternate suppliers (locally or online).

TANK
Red Heart® Super Saver®
Brown - #0360 Cafe Latte
White - #0311 White

DASH
Red Heart® Super Saver®
Lt Gray - #341 Light Gray
Blue - #885 Delft Blue
White - #311 White
Dk Gray - #3950 Charcoal

PRINCESS
Red Heart® Super Saver®
Cream - #0313 Aran
Pink - #0722 Pretty N' Pink
Brown - #0360 Cafe Latte
Dk Gray - #3950 Charcoal
Lt Gray - #0341 Light Gray
White - #0311 White

BUDDY
Premier® Pixie Dust® Brights
Tan - #2096-18 Toffee
White - #2096-06 White
Black - #2096-11 Black

JUNIOR PUP
Premier® Parfait® Chunky
Tan - #1150-41 Mushroom
Black - #1150-10 Black
Cream-#1150-07 Cream

DEXTER
Red Heart® Super Saver®
Brown - #0326 Oatmeal
Blue - #0381 Light Blue
Dk Gray - #3950 Charcoal
Burgundy - #0376 Burgundy
Pink - #0724 Baby Pink
White - #0311 White

MAX
Red Heart® Super Saver®
White - #0311 White
Green - #0661 Frosty Green
Black - #0312 Black
Lt Gray - #0341 Light Gray

BUSTER
Red Heart® Super Saver®
Tan - #0334 Buff
Brown - #0360 Cafe Latte
White - #0311 White
Dk Gray - #3950 Charcoal
Green - #0624 Tea Leaf

DOG PAW RUG
Bernat® Softee® Chunky™
Tan - #28021 Linen
Lt Brown - #28011 Soft Taupe
White - #28005 White

DOG BED
Lion Brand® Cover Story
220X Emery

BONE PILLOW
Premier® Snow Cone™ Light Chenille
Color A - #07 Root Beer
Premier® Basix™ Worsted
Color B - #44 Linen

"HOUNDS-TOOTH" FOODMAT
Bernat® Handicrafter® Cotton
Gray - #01042 Overcast
White - #01001 White

TOY BASKET
Lion Brand®
Feels Like Butta® Thick & Quick®
Lt Grey - #149AL Quiet Grey
Lt Green - #173B Willow

PUPPY LOVE BLANKET
Red Heart® Soft®
Blue - #4604 Navy
Brown - #9344 Chocolate
Off White - #4601 Off White

Production Team: Technical Editor – Linda A. Daley; Graphic Artist – Zachary Kline;
Editorial Editor & Photo Stylist – Shelbey Winningham; Photographer – Rob Karman.

We have made every effort to ensure that these instructions are accurate and complete.

Made in U.S.A.